WHICH DO YOU PREFER:
CHUNKY or
SMOOTH ?

WHICH DO YOU PREFER:
CHUNKY or SMOOTH ?

HEATHER BRAZIER

with illustrations by Rachel Parker

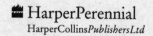
HarperPerennial
HarperCollins*Publishers*Ltd

Illustrations copyright © 1992 by Rachel Parker

First HarperPerennial edition: 1992

Canadian Cataloguing in Publication Data

Brazier, Heather, 1962-
Which do you prefer: chunky or smooth?

HarperPerennial ed.
ISBN 0-00-637919-2

1. Canada — Miscellanea. I. Title.
FC61.B73 1992   971.064'7'02   C92-094494-9
F1008.3.B73 1992

92 93 94 95 96 97 98 99 ❖ CCI 9 8 7 6 5 4 3 2 1

In memory of Diane Louise, my beloved
mother, my mentor, my very best friend

a'verage n. 1. generally prevailing rate, degree, or amount; ordinary standard; middle estimate (*on the* or *an, on, average*)

a'verage v.t. 1. estimate average of, especially as arithmetic mean; estimate general standard of; amount on an average to; do etc. on an average.

The Concise Oxford Dictionary of Current English

Contents
(a partial listing)

Acknowledgements

There are many people to whom I owe a great many thanks.

First, to David Colbert, who offered me the chance to write this book. I will never forget my surprise when David, responding to a request for some sort of do-at-home part-time proofreading job, called and asked if I'd be interested in doing some research. It wasn't until just before we signed off that I realized what this research was for: a book, and I would be its author!

To Laura Krakowec, my editor extraordinaire, thank you for your guidance, your skill, your concern and most of all your patience. You helped me transform a collection of unrelated facts and figures into a logical, readable order.

To Rebecca Vogan, my very adept copy editor, your little sticky notes of suggestions and comments, stuck in strategic locations throughout my manuscript, were invaluable. Thanks too for converting all my Imperial measures into metric, a system that still baffles me.

To Rachel Parker, my talented illustrator, your drawings are a delightful and important addition to the text.

To Mr. James Hall, Vice-President Business Publications, Maclean Hunter Limited, thank you for generously providing me with the vast array of magazines, which have been an invaluable source of information.

To the Staff and Residents of The Gage Transitional Living Centre. You have provided me with the opportunity to show myself that I am independent and able to tackle life's endless challenges.

To Doctors Joanne Bargman, Robert Inman, Michael Matthews, Tony Rebuck, Peter Webster and Tom Wright. Without your collective medical expertise, dedication and compassion I would not be here today.

To Anne Galbraith, Judy Gill, Ann Mandel, Michael Ondaatje and Skip Shand. Your friendship and encouragement in my educational endeavours from Grade 1 to my B.A. have instilled in me a love of language and literature.

To my dear friends Kay and Rachel Bassford, Nancy Beatty, Bryson Boright, Joe Burg, Del and Mike Burnet, Chris Dowson, Jennie and Theresa Evans, Yolanda Groenewoud, Rev. Bob Hunt, Linda Jackson, Marjorie Kuly, Winnie Osborne, Kate Parkinson, Robin Polson, Jeanne Schoolenberg, Linda Spalding and Irene Watpool. You are the ones that are always there to share in my joys and help me through my sorrows. Your friendship is a priceless gift.

To my very large family of aunts, uncles and assorted cousins. I am proud to proclaim there are too many of you to name individually. Each one of you is important to me, and to all of you I give a great big bear hug.

And as the saying goes, I've saved the best for last.
To my dear Dad, John Brazier, there are not enough words to express how much you mean to me.

Introduction

The word "average" is used to describe the middle of something or the typical someone. Average is neither the largest nor the smallest, the richest nor the poorest, the tallest nor the shortest, but somewhere in between.

Putting this book together was very much like working on a giant jigsaw puzzle. The outside edge of the puzzle is made up of pieces representing Canada as a country. The inside pieces are Canadians themselves and the things we do on an average day. These intricate interlocking pieces are all completely different, but when put together in their proper places, they form an original picture.

As your intrepid gatherer of vital and not-so-vital facts and figures, I had to begin by hunting for the hidden puzzle pieces. It became impossible to read the daily newspapers simply for current news and events. Any article that did not contain a number larger than 365, the criterion for a daily statistic, got passed over very quickly.

Suddenly, trade publications such as *Heavy Construction News* and the *Pulp and Paper Journal* became preferred reading. Many hours were spent on wild- (Canada) goose chases, looking for a particular fact and figure. Statistics Canada was an adventure in itself. A question such as how many fresh mushrooms are eaten in Canada, was answered with the total kilograms consumed by Canadians. Your faithful gatherer was then left to figure out how many individual mushrooms make up a kilogram. Thank goodness for calculators and rechargeable batteries!

One thing that has become very clear is that there really is no such thing as "an average day." Like people and snowflakes, no two days are exactly alike. It is this uniqueness that makes living in Canada and being Canadian so very special.

This is the kind of book that can never be completely finished. There will always be one more statistic to find. One more quirky fact to uncover. Infinite books to be written. What more could an author ask for!

H.B.
August 1992

HOW CANADIANS SPEND AN AVERAGE DAY

on an average day...

where time goes

...Employed men spend:

35 minutes washing and dressing
53 minutes preparing meals and doing housework
1 hour and 21 minutes eating
30 minutes getting to and from their activities
7 hours and 4 minutes at their salaried jobs
11 minutes expanding their knowledge by learning something new
22 minutes reading
39 minutes shopping
15 minutes looking after their children
10 minutes volunteering their time to help others or engaging in religious pursuits
2 hours and 8 minutes watching television
59 minutes socializing with friends and/or family
35 minutes participating in sports and hobbies
25 minutes being intimate with their significant other
7 hours and 53 minutes sleeping

WHICH DO YOU PREFER: CHUNKY OR SMOOTH?

on an average day...

...Employed women spend:

51 minutes washing and dressing

1 hour and 53 minutes preparing meals and doing housework

1 hour and 15 minutes eating

28 minutes getting to and from their activities

5 hours and 49 minutes at their salaried jobs

12 minutes expanding their knowledge by learning something new

19 minutes reading

54 minutes shopping

27 minutes looking after their children

16 minutes volunteering their time to help others or engaging in religious pursuits

1 hour and 31 minutes watching television

1 hour and 5 minutes socializing with friends and/or family

29 minutes participating in sports and hobbies

25 minutes being intimate with their significant other

8 hours and 6 minutes sleeping

on an average day...

...Unemployed men and women spend:

38 minutes washing and dressing

3 hours and 44 minutes preparing meals and doing housework

1 hour and 39 minutes eating

9 minutes getting to and from their activities

22 minutes looking for work

10 minutes expanding their knowledge by learning something new

26 minutes reading

1 hour and 15 minutes shopping

1 hour and 3 minutes looking after their children

22 minutes volunteering their time to help others or engaging in religious pursuits

1 hour and 31 minutes watching television

2 hours and 29 minutes socializing with friends and/or family

58 minutes participating in sports and hobbies

31 minutes being intimate with their significant other

8 hours and 37 minutes sleeping

on an average day...

...Employed Canadians spend:

10 hours and 24 minutes on personal care
9 hours and 6 minutes on productive time
4 hours and 30 minutes on free time

...Those keeping house spend:

11 hours and 24 minutes on personal care
9 hours and 6 minutes on productive time
4 hours and 30 minutes on free time

...Students spend:

10 hours and 54 minutes on personal care
8 hours and 12 minutes on productive time
4 hours and 54 minutes on free time

---

on an average day...

...Those looking for paid work spend:

11 hours and 42 minutes on personal care
4 hours and 24 minutes on productive time
7 hours and 42 minutes on free time

...Retired Canadians spend:

12 hours and 24 minutes on personal care
3 hours and 30 minutes on productive time
8 hours and 6 minutes on free time

...All other individuals spend:

12 hours and 36 minutes on personal care
4 hours and 24 minutes on productive time
7 hours on free time

on an average day...

...Excluding personal care activities, retired men living alone spend 10 hours and 36 minutes by themselves, more than any other group

...Their female counterparts spend 9 hours and 48 minutes alone

...We spend 20 minutes staring aimlessly into space (daydreaming)

special days

...72,685 Canadians celebrate their birthday

...If Christmas cards were purchased throughout the year, Canadians would spend an average of $2,191,781 a day on such cards

...17,548 of the cards would be UNICEF Christmas cards

on an average day...

...Canadians buy 219,178 roses, the favourite colour being red

...Depending on the city where the order is placed, the average cost of sending a dozen long-stemmed roses is as follows:

Halifax: $46.50
Montreal: $45.00
Ottawa: $50.50
Toronto: $48.00
Calgary: $53.90
Vancouver: $45.99
Whitehorse: $88.40

on an average summer day

...More than 3 million gas barbecues are in use across the country

on an average day...

on an average St. Patrick's Day

...25,000 people watch the annual parade through the streets of Toronto; it is the third largest St. Patrick's Day parade after Dublin, Ireland, and New York City

on an average Valentine's Day

...5 million roses are sold and 60 million Valentines are sent

on an average day...

here comes the bride

...522 marriages are performed

...The five most popular months for weddings are May, June, July, August and September. On an average day during these months, the following number of weddings take place:

May: 629
June: 744
July: 933
August: 870
September: 860

...The Canadian wedding industry, including such businesses as catering, rental halls, florists and formal wear, is worth $10,684,931

...The average cost of a wedding in Canada is $15,000

...Married couples pay $15,342,465 more in income taxes than they would if they lived common-law

on an average day...

keeping the faith

on an average (Sun)day:

...8,580,000 Canadians go to church

Of the total,

4,118,400 of the churchgoers are over age 65
2,059,200 are between 18 and 29 years of age
3,689,400 are Catholic
2,745,600 are Protestant
Attendance is lowest in British Columbia, with 1,801,800 attending
Quebeckers are most likely to attend church services, with 3,088,800 attending

...One Canadian enters the Hockley Valley Cistercian Monastery for a 5-day retreat
...The monastery's main source of income comes from the 274 pounds of fruitcake the monks bake daily

DAILY
DIVERSIONS

on an average day...

between the covers

...**164 new books are published in Canada, of which, 17 are by Canadian authors**

...**The federal government collects $821,918 from the GST on reading material**

...**14,603 Canadians read a book from cover to cover**

...**457,562 books are borrowed from the public library system**

on an average day...

...At least one specific request is made to public library staff to remove or restrict access to certain titles or subjects

...The Metro Toronto Reference Library, the largest public library in Canada, answers 3,836 telephone queries

...164 blind Canadians use the services provided by the Canadian National Institute for the Blind's braille, large-print and audio library

...The World's Biggest Bookstore in Toronto sells 115 self-help books

...26,575 Harlequin Romance novels are purchased

on an average day...

...Canada's largest detective bookstore, The Sleuth of Baker Street in Toronto, sells 164 new and used whodunits

...41 copies of the celebrated French dictionary, *Le petit Larousse en couleur*, are purchased
...37 of the copies are purchased in Quebec

...One of Canada's favourite children's authors, Robert Munsch, sells 8,219 copies of his books

...The Canadian Bible Society distributes and sells:
...685 complete Bibles
...959 copies of the New Testament
...548 portions of the Bible such as the Psalms and Gospels

...The literary arts receive $779,500 from the federal government

on an average day...

the fourth estate

...17,810,000 Canadians buy a
newspaper

on an average (week)day:

...Of newspapers with daily circulations of 100,000 or
more:

511,696 Canadians buy the *Toronto Star*, Canada's
largest newspaper
322,684 buy the *Globe and Mail*
294,563 buy *Le Journal de Montréal*
275,464 buy the *Toronto Sun*
197,255 buy *La Presse*
195,630 buy the *Vancouver Sun*
187,171 buy the *Vancouver Province*
177,188 buy the *Ottawa Citizen*
174,514 buy the *Montreal Gazette*
166,661 buy the *Edmonton Journal*

on an average day...

161,733 buy the *Winnipeg Free Press*
136,936 buy the *Hamilton Spectator*
125,234 buy the *Calgary Herald*
125,025 buy the *London Free Press*
105,842 buy *Le Soleil*
101,897 buy *Le Journal de Québec*

...The *Toronto Star* receives 2,000 telephone calls and enquiries

on an average (Sun)day:

...6,000 Torontonians buy the Sunday *New York Times*

on an average day...

keeping tabs on the tabloids

...42,857 Quebeckers buy their province's scandal week-lies, which focus on Quebec's homegrown stars
...The most popular, *Échos Vedettes*, sells 22,857 copies

...114,286 Canadians buy the *National Enquirer;* only 7,143 copies are sold in Quebec

...35,714 copies of the three weekly crime tabloids, *Âllo Police*, *Photo Police* and *Hebdo Police*, are sold in Quebec

the glossies

...116,516 Canadians buy *TV Guide* magazine

on an average day...

...43,006 copies of *Reader's Digest* are purchased
...30,709 Canadians purchase *Chatelaine* magazine
  (English edition)
...7,274 copies of *Châtelaine* (French edition) are sold
...19,095 copies of *Canadian Living* are purchased
...85,529 Canadians buy *Maclean's* magazine
...50,939 purchase the Canadian edition of *Time* magazine

...16,566 people read a copy of *Croc*, a Quebec-based French-language humour magazine, one of Canada's bestselling magazines in either language

comic relief

...14,521 Archie, Veronica and Jughead comic books are purchased

on an average day...

TV times

...We buy 3,836 colour televisions and 22 projection televisions

...Canadian adults watch 3 hours and 20 minutes of television

...Preschoolers watch 4 hours of television

...Elementary school children watch 2 hours and 55 minutes of television; they receive 2 hours and 30 minutes of classroom instruction

...Teenagers watch 3 hours of television

...Men watch 2 hours and 36 minutes of television

...Women watch 2 hours and 6 minutes of television

on an average day...

...A television viewer sees 55 commercials representing 36 minutes in a typical evening's worth of viewing

...As many as 200,000 Canadians watch MuchMusic at any given moment

...7 million Canadian households watch cable television

...Canadian cable television companies sign up 855 new subscribers

...The broadcasting industry receives $3,195,900 from the federal government

on an average day...

live theatre

...During its seven-month season, the Shakespearean Festival in Stratford, Ontario, attracts 2,239 people to a play in one of 3 theatres

...During its season, the Shaw Festival in Niagara-on-the-Lake, Ontario, draws 1,146 theatregoers

Phantom unmasked

...3,562 people attend the Toronto production of Andrew Lloyd Webber's *Phantom of the Opera*

...62 people watch the performance from the standing room area of the theatre

...140 students attend special Wednesday matinee performances

...$140,575 is taken in at the box office

...36 glasses of champagne are sold in the theatre lobby at $10 a glass

...27 chocolate truffles are purchased at $2 apiece

...$27,397 is spent on advertising the show

...821 theatregoers purchase either the CD or cassette of *Phantom* music

on an average day...

...2 hours are spent applying the Phantom's make-up

...1 tub of cold cream and 2 cakes of pancake make-up are used per performance

...4 pairs of pointe shoes need to be replaced after each performance

...29 pairs of tights, 17 white T-shirts, 23 white dress shirts must be laundered for each performance

...233 costume changes are made by the 40-member cast

at the movies

...205,321 people go to a movie theatre

...Box offices take in $958,904

private screenings

...Canadians buy 2,918 videocassette recorders

...Canadians buy 679 camcorders

on an average day...

...Canadians rent 958,904 videos worth $3,287,671
...Canadians buy $547,945 worth of pre-recorded videos

...822 films and 274 videos are rented through the National Film Board
...71 films are sold to the public by the National Film Board, 27 of which are copies of *Growing Up*, a three-part series on sex education for children age 9 to 12, available in English or French
...14 telecasts of National Film Board films are shown on CBC, TVOntario and Vision TV

...The federal government spends $46,575 on the production of its "home movies"; one of these films is titled *Where Your Tax Dollars Go*

...The film and video industry receives $452,900 from the federal government

on an average day...

music to the ears

...Canadians purchase $1,986,301 worth of recorded music

Of the total,

8 vinyl LP records are purchased
78,808 pre-recorded cassettes, worth $640,863 are purchased
4,521 compact disc players are purchased
64,479 compact discs worth $524,324 are purchased

...384 Canadians buy a copy of one of The Doors' original record albums from the 1960s

Of the total buyers,

68 choose *L.A. Woman*
41 choose *The Doors*
22 choose *Soft Parade*

...The sound-recording industry receives $10,300 from the federal government

on an average day...

aiding the arts

...The Canada Council receives $290,411 from the federal Department of Communications

...The Council awards $268,493 in grants to 3 artists and 8 arts organizations

...Canadian corporations donate $191,781 to the arts

it's worth a gamble

...$28,082,191 is spent by Canadians on legal gambling

...Canadians spend $9,589,041 on lottery tickets

on an average day...

...$3,615,342 worth of lottery tickets is sold in Ontario
...$1,879,178 is given back to players in winnings

...1,096 visitors gamble at Canada's first permanent legal
casino, Crystal Casino, in Winnipeg, Manitoba
...The casino takes in $175,342 in lost bets

...The Manitoba Lotteries Foundation generates:
$117,808 from the sale of lottery tickets
$35,616 from its Crystal Casino
$13,699 from government-run bingo halls

...33,973 people go to Canadian horse-racing tracks

THE PERSONALS

on an average day...

untying the knot

...214 Canadians are granted a divorce

Of the total divorces,

72 marriages dissolve after a separation of not less than three years

56 marriages dissolve because of adultery

48 marriages dissolve because of mental cruelty

28 marriages dissolve because of physical cruelty

2 marriages dissolve because of addiction to alcohol

8 marriages dissolve because of other grounds

playing it safe

...1.5 million Canadian women use The Pill

on an average day...

...134,962 condoms are purchased; 72,860 by women
...3,120,000 Canadians are allergic to the latex in condoms and end up with a very itchy rash

...164 men undergo a vasectomy

...110 women have a hysterectomy

an effort in fertility

...An average adult male produces 30 million sperm

...1,370 couples seek medical help for infertility

on an average day...

...137 men seek help from fertility clinics

abortion facts

...258 abortions are performed
Of the total,

195 abortions are performed in Canadian hospitals
59 abortions take place in free-standing clinics
4 women seek abortions in the United States

...Of the women who receive an abortion,
168 have never been married
59 are married
31 are divorced or widowed
57 are under age 20
139 are in their twenties
57 are in in their thirties
5 are in their forties

on an average day...

STDs

...208 people pick up one or more sexually transmitted diseases

...88 new cases of Chlamydia, the most common sexually transmitted disease, are diagnosed

how embarrassing

...13,699 Canadians discover they have a wart

THE PRICE OF BEAUTY

on an average day...

make-up

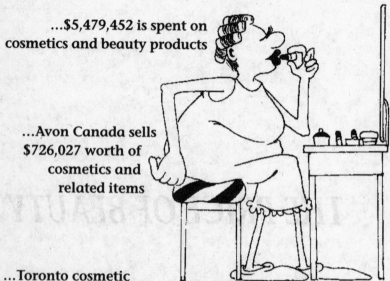

...$5,479,452 is spent on cosmetics and beauty products

...Avon Canada sells $726,027 worth of cosmetics and related items

...Toronto cosmetic maker Make-Up Art Cosmetics Ltd. (MAC) sells $68,493 worth of products. It counts Oprah Winfrey, Cher, Whitney Houston, Audrey Hepburn, Madonna and Princess Diana as its "most glamorous customers."

...Canadians buy $438,356 worth of antiperspirants and deodorants

on an average day...

makeover

...Before the ban was imposed, 35 women received a silicone breast implant

...110 Canadians have fat surgically removed; 22 are men

...$82,191,780 is spent on cosmetic surgery
...178 Canadians undergo cosmetic surgery; 27 of them are men
...Men have 30% of all nose jobs, 50% of pinning back of ears, 25% of chin augmentations

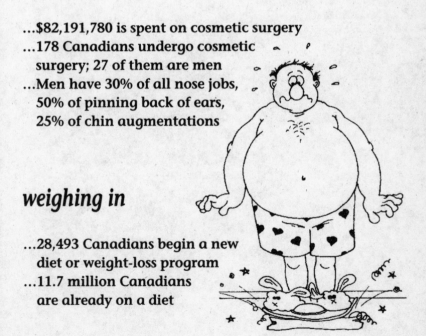

weighing in

...28,493 Canadians begin a new diet or weight-loss program
...11.7 million Canadians are already on a diet

on an average day...

...We spend $1,095,890 on fees payable to weight-loss clinics and the special food products these clinics sell

...The Canadian diet industry takes in $821,918 from diet-related services and specialty products

...Canadians buy $273,973 worth of specialty diet foods

WE ARE WHAT WE EAT

on an average day...

Canada's Food Guide

...Canada's Food Guide recommends that we eat:

2 servings from the milk and dairy products group
2 servings from the meat, fish and poultry group
3 servings from the bread and cereals group
4 servings from the fruit and vegetable group

...It costs $19.35 to feed a family of four

the egg comes first

...We use 15,631,200
fresh eggs

on an average day...

meat market

...Canadians eat:

2,706,849 kilograms of beef
2,136,986 kilograms of pork
1,638,356 kilograms of chicken

the dairy case

...Canadians consume 275,669 kilograms of butter

...Canadians consume 300,639 kilograms of cheddar cheese

...Canadians consume 197,764 kilograms of processed cheese

on an average day...

...Canadians consume 84,898 kilograms of cottage cheese

...Canadians buy 1,320,000 individual containers of yogurt

getting our veggies

...Canadians consume 4,042,466 kilograms of fresh vegetables

For example, we eat:

...142,295 kilograms of fresh broccoli—about 620,000 bunches

...226,378 kilograms of mushrooms—approximately 14,959,000 individual mushrooms

bringing home the bacon

...Canadians buy $121,203,300 worth of groceries

on an average day...

...33 new food products are introduced to the Canadian marketplace

...Canadians buy $208,219 worth of certified organic food products; $145,753 worth is imported

...Canadians buy $170,959 worth of Mexican foods

...We buy $136,986 worth of kosher foods

...46,544 bottles of barbecue sauce are sold

on an average day...

...Canadians purchase 12,537 packages of rice cakes

...Canadians eat 5,128,767 bananas

...Campbell Soup's plant in Chatham, Ontario, produces 78,912 284 ml cans of tomato soup

...Canada Packers sells 8,219 packages of their deli-sliced cold cuts

...Monarch Fine Foods plant in Rexdale, Ontario, produces 480,000 454 gram tubs/bricks of margarine

...Canadians purchase 21,918 Swanson TV dinners

on an average day...

sweet tooth

...Canadians consume 2,920,548 kilograms of sugar (most of it in processed foods)

...Canadian food producers use $68,493 worth of the artificial sweetener aspartame in their products

...Searle Pharmaceutical produces 328,767 Equal (Nutrasweet) sweetener tablets for Canadian use
...It exports 1,232,877 tablets to the United States

...$5,479,452 worth of bakery products is sold
...Voortman Bakery produces 8 million cookies in 60 varieties

on an average day...

...Saint Cinnamon Bake Shoppes produce 9,080 kilograms of their fat, gooey cinnamon buns

...We consume 80,849 kilograms of peanut butter
Of the total,

   20,212 kilograms are chunky
   60,637 kilograms are smooth
   Canadians choose smooth over chunky 3 to 1

...219,178 mason jars are used by Canadians keen on making their own jams, jellies and other preserves

more for your money

...186,575 kilograms of food additives and preservatives are added to Canadian-produced food products

on an average day...

we'll drink to that

...When Canadians are asked what they like to drink for breakfast,

9,620,000 choose water
9,100,000 drink coffee
2,860,000 prefer juice
1,820,000 sip tea
1,040,000 go for soda pop

...Canadians drink a total of 55,575,000 cups of coffee

...Canadians drink 7,764,384 litres of milk

...We buy 2,241,864 litres of bottled water, worth $556,164

on an average day...

...Quill Springs Mineral Water, bottled in Wynyard, Saskatchewan, from a natural mineral spring located under the warehouse floor, produces 80,000 litres of water

...The soft drink industry sells $9,041,096 worth of carbonated beverages

...2,191,781 soft drinks are sold in recycled plastic bottles

...26 million recyclable cans of soft drinks are consumed—one for each man, woman and child

...2,465,753 beverages are purchased in tetra pak drinking boxes

...Canadians in Quebec and the Maritimes purchase 30,000 bottles of Guy LaFleur's Flower Power fruit juice

on an average day...

...Athletic Canadians buy $191,781 worth of Gatorade

...We purchase $20,088 worth of instant iced tea mix

...VS Services, the leader in vending, foodservice management, health care foodservice and the largest employer of dieticians in Canada, serves 821,918 cups of coffee and uses 32,877 tea bags, giving it the title of "number one server of caffeine in Canada"

on an average day...

snack attack

...We consume 883,288 litres of ice cream
Of the total,
   600,000 litres are vanilla—$1,369,863 worth of ice cream

...Canadians eat 274,888 kilograms of chocolate—about
   4,840,000 regular-size chocolate bars

...17 million Rowntree Smarties are made

...183,561 Tootsie Rolls and Pops are sold

on an average day...

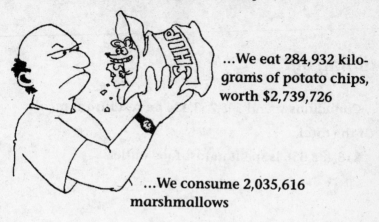

...We eat 284,932 kilograms of potato chips, worth $2,739,726

...We consume 2,035,616 marshmallows

...30,137 of Culinar's Vachon Jos. Louis cakes are purchased

...We buy 279,000 bags of cookies, 55,800 of which are chocolate chip

...10,908 packages of President's Choice Decadent Chocolate Chip Cookies are purchased—they are Canada's best-selling brand of cookies

on an average day...

dining out

...Canadians spend $65,753,424 on restaurant meals
Of the total,
   $16,438,356 is spent in fast-food outlets

...8,060,000 Canadians do not eat breakfast
...2,600,000 buy their breakfast in a restaurant or fast-food outlet

...Arby's sells 32,877 roast beef sandwiches, which require 2,985 kilograms of roast beef

...Dairy Queen restaurants sell 71,233 soft ice cream cones and use 669 kilograms of candy to make their Blizzards
...Dairy Queen takes in $509,589 in revenue

on an average day...

...Druxy's Restaurants sell 12,329 bagels

...Edo Japan, Canada's number-one Japanese restaurant chain, serves 1,057 kilograms of rice and goes through 1,309 litres of teriyaki sauce

...The Keg Restaurants serve up 6,849 steaks and 3,425 Caesar salads

...Kentucky Fried Chicken serves 986,301 pieces of chicken

...Manchu Wok, Canada's number-one Chinese food chain, does $273,973 worth of business

They sell:

6,219 kilograms of rice
24,658 egg rolls
32,877 chicken balls

on an average day...

...Mr. Submarine sells 54,795 subs—an average of 171 per store—worth $273,973

...Orange Julius uses 1,496 litres of orange juice to make their famous drink

...Pizza Pizza does $410,959 worth of business

They use:

7,123 kilograms of cheese
6,205 kilograms of dough
4,882 litres of tomato sauce
1,995 kilograms of pepperoni

...When Canadians are asked what they put on their pizza,

25,740,000 order mozzarella cheese
12,220,000 order mushrooms
11,960,000 order pepperoni
8,840,000 order green pepper

on an average day...

8,840,000 order bacon
6,500,000 order ham
4,420,000 order pineapple
3,120,000 order ground beef
2,600,000 order olives
234,000 order onions
208,000 order salami
130,000 order anchovies
104,000 order parmesan cheese
104,000 order sliced tomatoes
78,000 order sausage
52,000 order ricotta cheese

...Red Lobster Restaurants sell 2,488 kilograms of shrimp

...Tim Horton Donuts sell 2,739,726 donuts, cookies, muffins and cakes
...Their busiest store is in
Port Hope,
Ontario

on an average day...

...Yogen Fruz dishes up 6,530 kilograms of frozen yogurt

under the Golden Arches

...McDonald's Restaurants serve 22 million meals to 1.5 million customers

...We buy $6,575,342 worth of McDonald's food products

...McDonald's Restaurants of Canada's grocery bill comes to $1,369,863

They purchase:

63,014 kilograms of beef
54,795 kilograms of chicken
9,589 kilograms of pork
5,479 kilograms of fish
235,616 kilograms of potatoes
72,603 litres of milkshake and sundae mix

on an average day...

13,699 kilograms of cheese
986,304 buns
124,932 eggs

...The busiest McDonald's in Canada takes in $13,425 and is located at the intersection of highways 400 and 89, in Cookstown, Ontario

THE HEALTH OF
OUR NATION

on an average day...

health benefits

...Canadians spend $131,506,840 on health care

...The federal government spends $830,137 on medical research

...The provincial governments spend $402,740

...Non-profit organizations spend $367,123

...The pharmaceutical industry spends $783,562

...10,078 people are admitted to hospital; 5,543 of the admissions are senior citizens

...Only 200,000 of the 2,790,168 Canadians over the age of 65 are cared for in institutions

on an average day...

...The following takes place at the Hospital for Sick Children in Toronto, Ontario:

49 children are admitted, half of whom are from outside of Metro Toronto

740 outpatient visits are made to the many clinics run by the hospital

110 children are brought to the emergency room

36 children undergo a surgical procedure, 25 of whom return home the same night

2,740 meals are served out of the hospital kitchen

318 slices of pizza are served

858 Band-Aids are used

16 soothers are given to hospitalized infants

960 bags of intravenous solutions are used

12 litres of liquid soap are used

548 pairs of sterile disposable gloves are used

2,740 pairs of unsterile disposable gloves are used

12 requests for interpreting services are provided by volunteers fluent in 41 languages and dialects

what's up, doc?

...1 Canadian doctor gives up his or her practice and moves to the United States

on an average day...

...7 patients try to sue either a doctor, a hospital or other medical staff for malpractice
...1 patient is compensated

...Canadian doctors and hospitals spend $547,945 on medical malpractice insurance
...$68,493 is paid out to patients and their families as the result of malpractice or negligence by a Canadian doctor or hospital

take two aspirins...

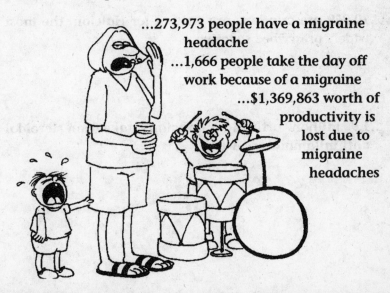

...273,973 people have a migraine headache
...1,666 people take the day off work because of a migraine
...$1,369,863 worth of productivity is lost due to migraine headaches

on an average day...

...Canadians spend $534,246 on non-prescription headache remedies

...2,739,726 Aspirin and generic ASA tablets are swallowed by Canadians

...528,767 prescriptions are written and filled

...10,959 prescriptions are written for Halcion, the most widely prescribed sedative

...1.9 million arthritic Canadians take non-steroidal anti-inflammatory drugs

on an average day...

illness, disease and disability

...164 Canadians are diagnosed with diabetes

...6 new cases of tuberculosis are diagnosed

...1 person comes down with bacterial meningitis
...9 are diagnosed with hepatitis B

...13 Canadians come down with whooping cough

...192 people are admitted to hospitals with flu-related illnesses
...14 will succumb to their illness

on an average day...

...Food poisoning costs the country $3,561,644 in lost wages, medical care and lost income from spoiled food

...192 calls are placed to the 24-hour poison control hotline at the Hospital for Sick Children in Toronto

...500,000 Canadians must cope with some obsessive-compulsive disorder

...3 Canadians become paralysed owing to a spinal cord injury

...According to the Canadian Chiropractic Association, back complaints cost the country $2,739,726 in lost wages, medical care and insurance claims

on an average day...

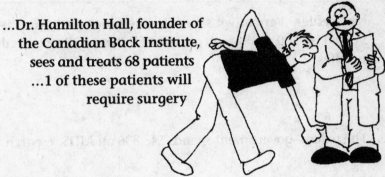

...Dr. Hamilton Hall, founder of the Canadian Back Institute, sees and treats 68 patients ...1 of these patients will require surgery

HIV and AIDS

...15 Canadians are told they are HIV-positive
...2 people are diagnosed with AIDS
...1 person dies from the disease

...Canadian blood labs test 205 specimens for the AIDS virus

...Toronto's AIDS needle exchange, called The Works, collects 75 used syringes
...The Works gives away 111 condoms to its clients

on an average day...

...McNeedles, Vancouver's needle exchange program, is visited by 500 customers and distributes 1,333 sterilized needles

...The federal government spends $43,836 on AIDS research

surgical manoeuvres

...6,158 people undergo surgery

...49 Canadians break a hip

...55 Canadians undergo hip replacement surgery

...274 Canadians have a cataract removed, artificial lenses implanted or retinas/corneas repaired

on an average day...

medical supplies and devices

...We use $2,739,726 worth of medical supplies

...Canadians buy $2,739,726 worth of incontinence products

...Denture wearers spend $41,096 on pastes and powders to make their plates fit more snugly

...973,800 Canadians use a hearing aid

HAZARDOUS HABITS

on an average day...

...Substance abuse costs the economy $7,123,288

straight up or on the rocks?

...We consume
5,567,562 litres of
alcoholic beverages

...Canadians buy
$27,397,260
worth of beer,
wine and spirits

...When Canadians over the age of 14 are asked if they
consume alcohol:

1,338,810 say they never drink
3,184,745 say they have given up alcohol
15,761,445 drink occasionally
2,080,000 Canadians drink at least one alcoholic beverage
every day

on an average day...

...Canadians drink 194,520 bottles of wine

...$630,137 worth of Ontario wine is sold across the country

...Canadians buy 369,863 one-litre bottles of hard liquor

...46,032 one-litre bottles of Seagram's Canadian whiskey are sold

...15,419 bottles of Hiram Walker's Canadian Club whiskey are sold

on an average day...

...We consume 16,438,356 bottles of domestic beer and 65,753 bottles of non-alcoholic beer, worth $23,835,616

...Canadians buy 65,748 bottles of low-alcohol beer (0.5%) and have 20 brands to choose from

...$547,945 worth of Canadian beer is sold in the United States

...$82,192 worth of American beer is sold in Canada

...The Moosehead Breweries plant in Saint John, New Brunswick, fills 2,364,480 beer bottles, making them the fastest operation to fill individual bottles in the world

on an average day...

...49,315 bottles of Beer, a generic brand made by the Drummond Brewing Company of Red Deer, Alberta, are sold

...156 bottles of Pride Beer, a brew specifically targetted at the gay and lesbian community, are sold by Brick Brewing Company Ltd., of Waterloo, Ontario. The beer is the brainchild of Toronto bar owner, Robert Amyotte. The gay and lesbian community receives a percentage of the sales.

...5,479 cases of liquor are smuggled across the border from the United States
...Most of these 49,311 bottles cross the border hidden in the luggage of Canadians

...4,750 meetings of Alcoholics Anonymous are held
...2,000 meetings of Al-Anon are held

on an average day...

...325 Canadians are charged with impaired driving

Of the total,

296 are men, 110 of whom are between the ages of 25 and 34

...The number of impaired driving charges per province is as follows:

British Columbia: 37
Alberta: 49
Saskatchewan: 20
Manitoba: 14
Ontario: 104
Quebec: 65
New Brunswick: 11
Nova Scotia: 12
Prince Edward Island: 2
Newfoundland: 8
Yukon: 1
Northwest Territories: 1

...3 Canadian babies are born with some degree of fetal alcohol syndrome

on an average day...

...223 Canadians give up drinking alcoholic beverages

...115 persons are treated for alcohol-related problems in hospital emergency rooms

...52 Canadians die as a direct result of alcohol use

illegal substances

...When Canadians over the age of 14 are asked if they use illegal drugs:

1,318,525 currently use marijuana or hashish
283,990 use cocaine or crack

on an average day...

...33,334 Canadians use a narcotic obtained illegally, usually from prescriptions written by unsuspecting doctors

...174 people are charged with a drug offence:

	Total Charges	Possession	Trafficking	Importing	Growing
Heroin	3	1	1	1	
Cocaine	43	16	21	6	
Marijuana	106	75	27	1	3

...$860,274 worth of cocaine, hash oil and marijuana is confiscated by Canada Customs drug agents at Canadian airports and border crossings

on an average day...

...9 Young Offenders are charged with a drug offence

...1 Canadian dies as a result of an overdose of illegal drugs

...Only 200 spaces are available in Ontario for heroin addicts needing daily doses of methadone to help them kick their habit

...1,200 spaces are available in British Columbia

the smoking section

...The Canadian tobacco industry takes in $22,465,753

...The Canadian tobacco industry spends $273,973 on advertising

on an average day...

...5.4 million Canadians smoke

...Canadian youths spend $1,095,890 on tobacco products

...329 children, age 18 and under, will take up smoking, 230 of them before the age of 16

...32,876,712 cigarettes are produced

...28,767,121 of these cigarettes are sold and smoked in Canada; the remaining 4,109,591 are exported

Of the cigarettes exported,

3,287,672 of them go to the United States

410,959 are put on airlines and ships, are given to diplomats and are sold to Europe

410,960 are shipped to St. Pierre-Miquelon

on an average day...

...760,500 cigars are produced

...The federal government gleans $6.8 million in taxes from the sale of cigarettes

...32,877 cartons of cigarettes are smuggled into Canada; 9,863 cartons are American brands
...6,849 cartons of Marlboro cigarettes (1,369,863 cigarettes) are sold illegally in Canada
...The federal government loses $1,013,699 in taxes normally collected on these cigarettes

...Canada's major tobacco firm, Imasco Ltd., owner of Imperial Tobacco Ltd., gives:

$1,712 to the University of Toronto
$1,546 to health care facilities
$407 to health-related charities
$274 to the Toronto Hospital
$137 to Montreal's Institute of Cardiology
$411 to the Ontario Cancer Care Fund
$51 to the Canadian Red Cross Society

on an average day...

...Canadian doctors write 959 prescriptions for Nicorette, to help their patients quit smoking

...334 Canadians quit smoking

...104 Canadians die from the effects of smoking

A MATTER OF
LIFE AND DEATH

on an average day...

arrivals

...1,123 babies are born in Canada
...243 of these babies are born to unwed mothers
......463 are born to first-time mothers

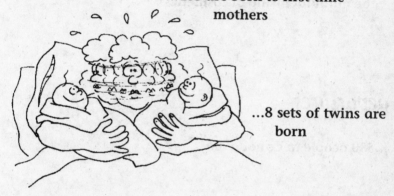

...8 sets of twins are born

...4 stillbirths occur

...3 women under the age of 15 give birth
...4 women over the age of 40 give birth

...5 infants are adopted through public adoption services

on an average day...

...After childbirth, the placentas from 438 Canadian women are sold by hospitals for 35 cents each to Bocknek Ltd., a Toronto-based animal by-products company that sells the tissue to Institut Merieux, a pharmaceutical company in Lyons, France for use in the manufacturing of cosmetics

departures

...530 people in Canada die

...10 people in Canada commit suicide—7 male, 3 female
...3 of the suicides occur in Quebec

...1 teenager commits suicide
...224 teenagers try to take their own life

on an average day...

...160 people are cremated
...327 people are buried

...$66,027 worth of coffins and caskets is sold

the five leading causes of death in Canada

heart disease (1)

...219 Canadians die from heart disease

...247 Canadians suffer a heart attack
...137 of the attacks are fatal

...The federal government spends $35,616 on research into heart disease

---

on an average day...

cancer (2)

...158 Canadians lose their lives to cancer
...307 new cases of cancer are diagnosed

...47 new cases of lung cancer are diagnosed
...39 people die from lung cancer

...28 men are diagnosed with prostate cancer
...9 men die from the disease

...38 women are diagnosed with breast cancer
...14 women die from the disease

...126 Canadians are diagnosed with skin cancer
...8 of these people have the most deadly form of melanoma
...2 people lose their life to the disease

on an average day...

...Canadians spend $123,288 on 24,658 bottles of sunscreen products to protect their skin

strokes (3)

...137 Canadians suffer a stroke
...38 of the strokes are fatal

respiratory diseases (4)

...43 Canadians die from a respiratory disease, most of which are caused by smoking-related illnesses

...1 person dies from asthma

on an average day...

accidents (5)

...26 Canadians die as a result of an accident

...12 Canadians are killed in a traffic-related accident
Of the total deaths,

   5 occur during daylight hours
   3 occur after dark
   4 occur at 4:30 p.m.

...Lives lost to other leading causes of accidental death
   are as follows:

   5 people die from accidental falls
   1 person drowns
   1 person succumbs to injuries from accidental fires
   1 person chokes to death
   1 person dies from poisoning

...7 left-handed Canadians die as a result of an accident
   involving a product designed for right-handed people

on an average day...

...10,959 Canadians are injured in an accident

giving and receiving the gift of life

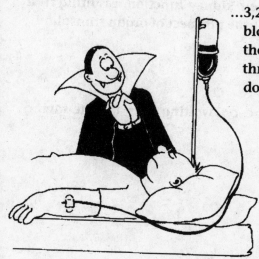

...3,221 pint-sized bags of blood are collected by the Canadian Red Cross through their blood donor clinics
...321 of these pints are discarded by the Red Cross Society because of the proven or suspected presence of disease

...4,320 Canadians need a blood transfusion

on an average day...

...3 people receive a new chance at life through the gift of a donated organ—kidneys, hearts, livers, lungs and corneas

...6 Canadians lose their kidney function, resulting in a lifetime of dialysis or the prospect of organ transplant

...1,520 Canadians are on waiting lists for life-saving organ transplants

PERSON TO PERSON

on an average day...

telephone directory

...98,630,136 local telephone/fax calls are made

...5,479,452 long-distance telephone/fax calls are placed

...Canadians buy 485 cellular telephones

...384 Canadians subscribe to a cellular phone service

...600,000 Canadians use their car cellular phone at least once

...667 calls to 911 are made using a car cellular phone

on an average day...

...1,877 cordless telephones are purchased
...2,685 telephone answering machines are sold

...The Hospital for Sick Children in Toronto receives 120 calls from across Canada to its 24-hour medical information service

...The Metro Toronto Distress Centre receives 125 calls

...The Better Business Bureau receives 1,762 consumer complaints, requests and enquiries

...Canada's largest university, the University of Toronto, receives 1,500 telephone calls through its main switchboard

on an average day...

...The free legal service offered by the Law Society of Upper Canada receives 411 calls

...Canadians buy $21,369,863 worth of products that are offered to them through telephone sales

...Telemarketing costs Canadians $54,795 in fraudulent sales and claims

...143,334 people receive their phone bill from Bell Canada

on an average day...

Canada's post

...Canada Post delivers
26,575,342
pieces of
addressed mail

This total consists of:

16,082,191 pieces of
letter mail
8,493,151 pieces of
junk mail
1,600,000
publications
200,000 parcels
100,000 pieces of special delivery mail
100,000 pieces of free parliamentary mail

...82,192 parcels enter Canada

Of the total,

49,315 are destined for the average Canadian, while the remainder go to businesses and other commercial destinations
8,219 are inspected by Canada Customs
4,110 are subjected to duty, excise tax and/or the GST

---

on an average day...

...United Parcel Service (UPS) delivers 100,000 packages and parcels, taking in $424,658 in revenue

...Canada Post issues 4,794,520 general issue stamps and 205,548 individual commemorative stamps

LEARNING AND LITERACY

on an average day...

learning our lessons

...$127,345,200 is spent on education

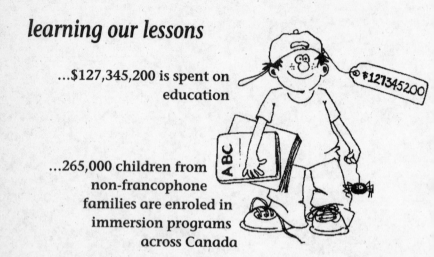

...265,000 children from non-francophone families are enroled in immersion programs across Canada

...274 high school students drop out

...High school drop-outs cost the economy $8,219,178 in unemployment insurance and social welfare benefits

...The federal government spends $15,068 on an advertising campaign to encourage kids to "Stay in School"

...136 students drop out of apprenticeship programs

...1,370 Canadian students compete in their school's science fair

on an average day...

...Students spend more than twice as much time with friends than the average Canadian 15 years of age and over—5 hours and 12 minutes, compared to 2 hours and 24 minutes

...Male students spend 6 hours and 30 minutes on their studies
...Female students spend 6 hours on their studies

...152 women earn an undergraduate degree
...20 women earn a master's degree
...2 women earn a Ph.D.
...132 men earn an undergraduate degree
...25 men earn a master's degree
...5 men earn a Ph.D.

...Graduates with a bachelor's degree earn $86
...Those with a master's degree earn $102
...Doctoral graduates earn $162

on an average day...

...26 adults and 6 young people are enroled in the National Circus School–L'École Nationale de Cirque, in Montreal, Quebec

...15 would-be shepherds are enroled in a 17-week training course at British Columbia's Okanagan College

...1,534 people learn cardio-pulmonary resuscitation (CPR)

...8 people graduate from the Canadian Institute of Hamburgerology

on an average day...

words without meaning

...4 million Canadians deal with their own functional illiteracy

...Illiteracy costs the country $27,397,260

...$10,958,904 is lost by businesses because of the illiteracy of some of their employees

...As the result of illiteracy in Canada:

1,560,000 people cannot circle the expiry date on a driver's licence

2,600,000 are unable to read the directions on a bottle of medication

2,860,000 cannot read a highway traffic sign

7,540,000 are unable to circle the amount owing on a telephone bill

13,000,000 cannot find a specific store in the Yellow Pages

18,200,000 cannot find an amount on the income tax table

CANADIANS IN NEED

on an average day...

poverty in Canada

...**3,129,000 Canadians, 1 in every 8, have incomes below the poverty line**
(Statistics Canada sets the poverty line using a standard that families or individuals who spend 58.5% or more of their pre-tax income on clothing and shelter are in financial difficulty. For example, the poverty line for a family of four living in a large Canadian city would be $67.69 per day. For a family of four living in a rural area it would be $49.79 per day.)

...**974,000 single Canadians live below the poverty line**

...**1,368,000 families exist below the poverty line**

...**1,166,000 children live below the poverty line**

on an average day...

feeding Canada's hungry

...19,573 Canadians must get their daily bread and other groceries from one of the country's 332 food banks

...The regional breakdown is as follows:

	TOTAL	INCLUDING (FROM TOTAL) CHILDREN UNDER AGE 18
Atlantic Provinces	1,873	880
Quebec	4,153	997
Ontario	9,167	3,575
Prairie Provinces	2,933	1,436
British Columbia	1,447	606

...6,333 children under the age of 18 rely on food from food banks

...Food banks distribute 62,192 kilograms of food

on an average day...

...There are 1,195 emergency grocery programs and 540 meal programs supplying 63,334 meals and 9,800 grocery hampers to hungry Canadians

the homeless

...125,000 Canadians make the streets their home

...100,000 runaway youths live on the streets of Canada's major cities

charities and volunteering

...4 new charities are started
...14,521 Canadians make a charitable donation
...$7,945,205 is given to charities by individuals
...$391,781 is given to charities by businesses

on an average day...

...Canada's 11.5 million Roman Catholics donate $4,932 to the Pope's Pastoral Works, commonly called the St. Peter's Pence Collection

...The United Way of Canada raises $572,602 through various fundraising events and donations

...Volunteers donate the equivalent of $32,876,712 in wages by providing their services and time to many causes
...Of Canada's 5.3 million dedicated volunteers, 2.9 million are women (55%), and 1 million are seniors

...The banking industry contributes $86,027 to Canadian charities
...The oil industry gives $63,562
...The beverage and tobacco industries donate $30,959
...Communications and telecommunications give $28,767
...Utilities contribute $26,575
...The primary metals industry gives $24,110

on an average day...

...Canadians volunteer 21,917 hours of their time to hospitals across the country

helping abroad

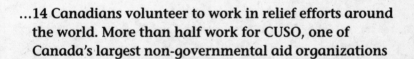

...274 Canadians become foster parents of a Third World child through Foster Parents Plan of Canada

...5 Canadians sponsor a Third World family

...14 Canadians volunteer to work in relief efforts around the world. More than half work for CUSO, one of Canada's largest non-governmental aid organizations

ALL OUR CHILDREN

on an average day...

child care

...Fathers spend:

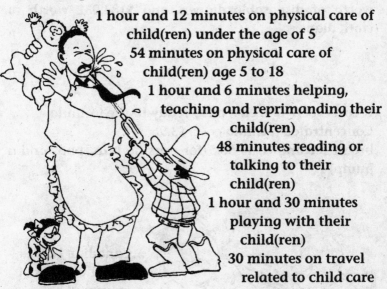

1 hour and 12 minutes on physical care of child(ren) under the age of 5

54 minutes on physical care of child(ren) age 5 to 18

1 hour and 6 minutes helping, teaching and reprimanding their child(ren)

48 minutes reading or talking to their child(ren)

1 hour and 30 minutes playing with their child(ren)

30 minutes on travel related to child care

...Mothers spend:

1 hour and 48 minutes on physical care of child(ren) under the age of 5

1 hour and 6 minutes on physical care of child(ren) age 5 to 18

48 minutes helping, teaching and reprimanding their child(ren)

48 minutes reading or talking to their child(ren)

1 hour and 18 minutes playing with their child(ren)

30 minutes on travel related to child care

on an average day...

baby talk

...Canadian baby bottoms are covered in $1,232,877 worth of disposable diapers and $184,932 worth of cloth diapers

...It costs $8.37 to feed a baby ready-to-use formula
...Concentrated formula costs $3.96
...breast feeding costs 56¢ (for nursing bras, pads and a pump)

...Canadian babies eat 641,096 jars of prepared baby foods and juices

...623,340 babies and toddlers spend their weekdays in a day-care centre

on an average day...

teen talk

...Canada's 2.5 million teenagers spend $16,438,356 ($6.57 each) on clothing, music, sporting goods, electronics and fast food

...Canadian teenagers spend $2,071,428 (83¢ each) on snack food

...52% of teenagers say their parents do not embarrass them
...70% have a high level of confidence in the police
...56% believe there's a God who looks after them
...23% believe their parents are too uptight about sex
...45% say Sears is where they shop most often
...50% of teenage girls age 12 to 14 are addicted to soap operas
...0% say they approve of cocaine or crack
...3% approve of marijuana
...57% of girls say they are under a great deal of stress
...43% of boys say they are under a great deal of stress
...92% say achievement in school is important to them

on an average day...

...110 teenagers get pregnant

...60 babies are born to teenage mothers
...54 of the babies are raised by their biological mothers

child's play

...$3,287,671 worth of toys is purchased

...366 toys are inspected by the
   Hazardous Products Department
...150 toys are
   deemed dangerous
   under the federal
   *Hazardous
   Products Act*

on an average day...

...Canada's only crayon manufacturer, Binney and Smith (Canada) Ltd., produces 1.15 million Crayola Crayons

They also produce:

120,548 felt marking pens
2,740 jars of children's poster paints
370 kilograms of clay

...They ship 175,342 crayons to the United States

...7,671,232 Lego bricks are sold
...50,000 Canadian children are members of the National Lego Club

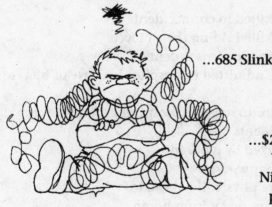

...685 Slinkys are purchased

...$273,973 worth of Teenage Mutant Ninja Turtle paraphernalia is sold

on an average day...

...Canadians buy $958,904 worth of video games
...Of the total, $767,123 is spent on Nintendo games

latch-key kids

...700,000 children come home from school to an empty
house

the perils of childhood

...4 children are killed in car accidents
...2 children are killed riding their bicycle
...41 are injured in bicycle accidents
...14 children are admitted to hospital because of bicycle
injuries
...822 children are taken to a hospital emergency room
because of accidents
...1 child is abducted by a parent
...191 children go missing
...274 children are physically abused
...137 teenagers run away from home

on an average day...

...1 child dies and 148 are accidentally injured owing to a defective consumer product

...5 children, age 4 and under are taken to a hospital emergency room because of accidents involving grocery carts

...1 child suffers from alcohol poisoning as a result of ingesting commercial mouthwash, some of which contain 30% alcohol

...3 children are killed because of accidents in the home

...76 confirmed cases of sexual assault involving juveniles occur
...In 39 of these cases, charges are laid
...30 of the confirmed cases involve children age 11 and under

on an average day...

...3 referrals are made to the Suspected Child Abuse and Neglect (SCAN) Program at Toronto's Hospital for Sick Children

...2 of these referrals are suspected cases of sexual abuse

our troubled youth

...4,000 juveniles are in jails, halfway houses or group homes

...32 youths are convicted and sentenced to one of these facilities

...65 girls age 12 to 17 are charged with *Criminal Code* offences

...295 boys age 12 to 17 are charged with *Criminal Code* offences

...6 girls are charged with assault

...15 boys are charged with assault

on an average day...

...439 federal statute charges are heard under the *Young Offenders Act*

...212 Young Offenders appear in federal court

...The Kids Help Phone receives 1,699 calls

Of the total,

764 calls are about interpersonal relationship problems

34 calls are about suicide

221 calls concern health-related problems, including abuse of drugs and/or alcohol

164 calls are about school problems

110 calls are from runaway kids

108 calls are about sexuality

153 are from victims of abuse and/or neglect

145 are from children troubled by divorce or domestic violence in the home

HOME SWEET HOME

on an average day...

the roof over our heads

...1,011 homes change ownership

...4 new co-op housing units are made available

...428 new homes are built

...8 houses are built and 11 are renovated on reserves across the country by Indian and Northern Affairs Canada

...Canadians owe $709,589,040 on their mortgages

on an average day...

...Canadians spend $61,369,863 on renovations to their homes and $2,739,726 on alterations to their apartments

creature comforts

...Canadians buy:

8,767 major appliances
2,805 sets of washers and dryers
2,323 microwave ovens

...Canadians buy $1,369,863 worth of small appliances that are made in 65 companies by 5,000 Canadian workers

...74 people invest in an automatic garage door opener

on an average day...

...$13,698,630 worth of furniture and home furnishings is purchased in Canada

...The La-Z-Boy factory in Waterloo, Ontario, makes 500 recliners, destined for every province and, it would seem, every living room in the country
...Canadians buy $1,726,027 worth of these chairs

...Canadians buy 1,584 gas barbecues

cleaning up

...Canadians buy $2,725,997 worth of household cleaning products
We buy:

207,288 boxes of laundry soap
94,145 bottles of dishwashing liquid
93,205 bottles of chlorine bleach

on an average day...

89,025 boxes of fabric softener sheets
49,408 abrasive cleansers
47,096 room deodorants
40,203 packages of dishwasher soap
29,939 toilet bowl cleaners
28,849 scouring pads with soap
22,510 bottles of glass cleaner
12,151 soapless scouring pads
10,756 bottles of furniture polish
10,016 bathroom cleansers
8,893 oven cleaners
8,663 cans of liquid floor wax
7,811 rug cleaners

brushing up

...We buy:

128,317 toothbrushes
70,622 paintbrushes
11,855 clothes brushes
6,812 brooms
2,561 mops
887 shoe brushes

on an average day...

pet projects

...4,053,000 Canadian households say they own a dog, cat, bird, fish or a combination

Of the total,

    2,205,000 own a dog
    2,044,000 own a cat
    7,432,000 own a bird, fish, rodent, snake or lizard or a combination of critters

...We spend $1,917,808 on pet food

Of the total,

    $901,369 is spent on canned gourmet cat food
    $575,342 is spent on high protein and special diet dog food

...Cat owners buy $82,192 worth of kitty litter
...Pet food companies spend $95,890 on advertisements for their products

...50% of Canada's dogs are overweight

on an average day...

...197 dogs are registered with the Canadian Kennel Club
Of the dogs registered,
...59 are purebred
...138 are of mixed breeds

...274 budgies are purchased in Toronto

...Of the 2,044,000 cats living in Canadian households,
1,022,000 of them started life as a stray

safety begins at home

...1,425 Canadians are injured in their own home

SPORTS AND
THE GREAT OUTDOORS

on an average day...

the sporting life

...Canadians purchase 70,208 pairs of athletic shoes worth $2,739,726

...56,166 pairs of these shoes will be worn by people who have no intention of exercising regularly

...Canstar Sports Group Inc. of Streetsville, Ontario, sells 3,562 pairs of hockey skates under the Bauer, Lange and Micron labels—more than any other company in the world. It supplies skates to 90% of NHL players.

...The Toronto Maple Leafs' president and general manager, Cliff Fletcher, earns $2,192—he is the NHL's highest paid executive
...Maple Leaf goalie Grant Fuhr earns $4,384—he is the league's highest paid goalie

on an average day...

...Whistler, British Columbia, plays host to 3,288 skiers, including 1,644 Canadians

...10,959 men and women play a round of golf

...Atomic Energy of Canada Ltd. laboratories in Pinawa, Manitoba, receives 720 golf balls a day to run through the centre's 10-million-volt nonradioactive electron beam accelerator, which alters the molecular core of the balls, supposedly improving their upshot, making them travel 18 to 27 metres farther

...Torpedo Inc. of Canada produces 493 premium quality toboggans

...Canadians buy 2,740 bicycles, 2,288 of which are imported

on an average day...

...The Rocky Mountain Bicycle Company of Richmond, British Columbia, sells 38 bikes at an average price of $793

...8,510,259 people ride a bicycle to work or school

...126 bicycle helmets are sold at discount prices through a joint effort between the Canadian Medical Association and Sandoz Pharmaceutical Canada Inc.

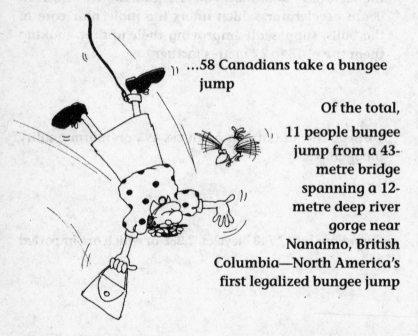

...58 Canadians take a bungee jump

Of the total, 11 people bungee jump from a 43-metre bridge spanning a 12-metre deep river gorge near Nanaimo, British Columbia—North America's first legalized bungee jump

on an average day...

...712 Canadians participate in paintball. The unusual field sport uses automatic rifles held by participants wearing face masks and goggles. They shoot one another with guns loaded with pellets of coloured paint: "splat, you die" is the object of the game.

...2,521 Canadians are injured while participating in a sport or leisure activity

at an average "home game"

...The Toronto Blue Jays lose 25 baseballs into the stands of the Skydome because of home runs and foul balls

on an average day...

...425 drivers drink too much at a Blue Jays home game and, if asked to take a breathalyzer test, would be charged with impaired driving

dawdling in dinghies

...Canadians purchase 115 pleasure boats, ranging from canoes to cabin cruisers, rubber rafts to yachts, with a total value of $991,781

...Various yacht club fees, not including initiation, add up to the following:

Royal Canadian Yacht Club, Toronto, Ontario	$4.36
Royal St. Lawrence Yacht Club, Dorval, Quebec	$2.41
Royal Nova Scotia Squadron, Halifax, N.S.	$1.92
Royal Kennebeccasis Yacht Club, Saint John, N.B.	$1.81
Royal Vancouver Yacht Club, Vancouver, B.C.	$1.51
Royal Victoria Yacht Club, Victoria, B.C.	$1.26

on an average day...

back to nature

...35,616 people visit one of Canada's National Parks

...26 hikers attempt to follow the West Coast Trail's 77-kilometre stretch of dense forest and rugged coastline between Port Renfrew and Bamfield in Pacific Rim National Park, on the west side of Vancouver Island
...Only 17 actually complete the course

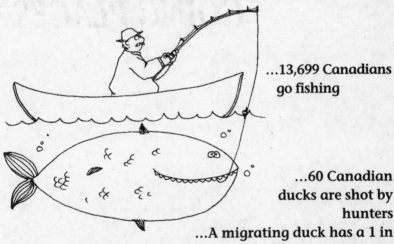

...13,699 Canadians go fishing

...60 Canadian ducks are shot by hunters
...A migrating duck has a 1 in 4 chance of survival—which is considerably worse than the average combat soldier

GOING PLACES

on an average day...

destination: Canada

...Tourism is Canada's fourth largest industry, generating $68,493,150 worth of business
Of the total, $13,698,630 belongs to the hotel industry

...295,890 people enter Canada via all forms of transportation

...The following number of tourists visit Canada:
95,162 Americans
1,532 Britons

on an average day...

1,132 Japanese
712 French
699 Germans
342 from Hong Kong
308 Dutch
307 Australians
175 Mexicans
109 Taiwanese
82 from the Commonwealth of Independent States
(formerly Russia)

...A family of four vacationing by car in Canada spends
$179.50 on food and lodgings—$95.40 on food, $84.10
on lodging

...47,123 people visit Toronto, Canada's number-one
tourist destination

Of those who come,

16,986 visit friends and/or relatives
15,890 come to see the sights
12,603 are on business
1,644 are attending a convention

on an average day...

travelling Canadians

...136,986 Canadians travel to the United States

...6,027 Canadians travel to Florida, our favourite American destination

Of the total,

3,797 of the travellers are from Ontario

2,411 drive to their destination

...Canadians spend $3,287,671 while in Florida

...The number of Canadians travelling abroad that go to:

Europe: 7,573

The Caribbean: 2,545

Central America: 1,408

Asia: 1,047

South America: 559

Australia/New Zealand: 359

Africa: 274

...Canadians spend $21,917,808 on business travel

on an average day...

...The Canadian Automobile Association receives 351 requests for TripTiks, which are individualized travel itineraries and route maps provided free of charge to members of the auto club

...518 other auto club members request literature packages to help them plan a trip

...137 of these literature packages contain information about Florida

...110 of the TripTiks are for Canadians travelling to Florida

...44,210 Canadians take a holiday within Canada

Of the total,

34,630 visit family and friends
2,740 go camping
2,137 visit another city

...438 Canadians go on a cruise

on an average day...

...2,693 Canadians take a gamble in Las Vegas

...143 Canadians visit the Yukon and Northwest Territories
...548 international visitors, including 510 from the United
States, go to the Yukon and Northwest Territories

...103 youth hostel memberships are purchased by students
wanting cheaper accommodation all over the world

checking in

...A top-of-the-line single occupancy hotel room costs:

$285 at the Hotel Vancouver
$260 at the Four Seasons Hotel, Toronto
$250 at the Château Laurier, Ottawa
$215 at the Ritz-Carlton, Montreal
$175 at the Sheraton Halifax
$155 at the Skyline Plaza Hotel, Calgary

on an average day...

...Room service prices across Canada for a cheese plate and a glass of Chardonnay at a first-class hotel:

	CHEESE	CHARDONNAY	TOTAL
Hotel Vancouver	$7.00	$6.00	$13.00
Four Seasons, Toronto	$7.00	$6.95	$13.95
Château Laurier, Ottawa	$8.50	$4.10	$12.60
Ritz-Carlton, Montreal	$12.00	$8.00	$20.00
Sheraton, Halifax	$13.12	$3.50	$16.62
Skyline Plaza, Calgary	$4.50	$4.50	$9.00
AVERAGE	$8.69	$5.51	$14.20

...Of Canada's 250,000 hotel rooms, 85,000 remain empty

...The kitchen of the Royal York Hotel in Toronto, the largest hotel kitchen in Canada,

provides room service to 1,600 rooms
serves 5,000 meals
makes 10 tonnes of ice cubes
brews 97 kilograms of coffee

on an average day...

recycles 7 tonnes of garbage using state-of-the-art machines
washes 2,000 dishes and 4,000 glasses every hour
spends $68,493.15 on food and beverages
sends 5,909 kilograms of organic waste (food leftovers and paper products) to the dump

...Toronto's Four Seasons Hotel uses:

2,286 individual bottles of shampoo
64 shower caps
41 boxes of tissue
167 rolls of toilet paper, which works out to 70,033 individual sheets or 8,005 metres

...The Empress Hotel in Victoria, British Columbia, serves 219 cups of tea at their 4:00 p.m. high tea

tourist traps

...1,918 people visit Green Gables, home of Anne, in Cavendish, Prince Edward Island

on an average day...

...156 attend the Charlottetown Theatre production of *Anne of Green Gables*

...$13,699 worth of Anne souvenirs is sold, including the books by Lucy Maud Montgomery

...55 people visit the Green Gables Museum on Prince Edward Island

...41 copies of the two-part video version of *Anne of Green Gables* are sold

...123 people visit the Canadian Museum of Caricature in Ottawa, Ontario

...Toronto's Casa Loma attracts 1,096 visitors

...3,640 people visit Toronto's CN Tower, the world's tallest free-standing structure

on an average day...

...Cullen Gardens Miniature Village, in Whitby, Ontario, draws 822 visitors (it's one of the most popular tourist attractions between Toronto and Montreal)

...Cullen Gardens sells $109,589 worth of plants, flowers and garden ware, and their mail-order catalogue receives orders worth $2,740

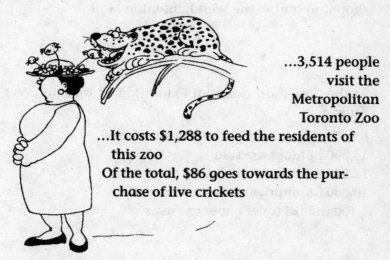

...3,514 people visit the Metropolitan Toronto Zoo

...It costs $1,288 to feed the residents of this zoo

Of the total, $86 goes towards the purchase of live crickets

...32,877 people visit the Canadian side of Niagara Falls

...237.6 billion litres of water flow over Niagara Falls

on an average day...

...The Royal Ontario Museum in Toronto receives 2,394 visitors

...60,000 visitors shop 'til they drop at Canada's largest shopping centre, the West Edmonton Mall

...At the Canadian National Exhibition in Toronto every August,

6,810 kilograms of garbage are collected
16,000 hotdogs are sold
12,500 orders of French fries are served
10,000 hamburgers are consumed
1,100 rolls of toilet paper are used

over the border

...12.3 million Americans visit Canada for less than 24 hours

on an average day...

...161,644 Canadians cross the American border by private car on a trip that will be shorter than 24 hours

...39,178 stay for 48 hours or longer

...15,000 private vehicles cross the Peace Bridge at Niagara Falls, heading into the United States

...Financial institutions in Port Colborne, one of Ontario's border towns near Niagara Falls, exchange $19,178 worth of Canadian currency into American money

...At a typical Bank of Montreal branch in St. Catharines, Ontario, $4,000 is exchanged into American funds

on an average day...

...Ontarians cross the border to fill up their vehicles with 821,918 litres of less expensive American gasoline

...Cross-border shopping costs the Canadian economy $9,589,041

PLANES, TRAINS AND AUTOMOBILES

on an average day...

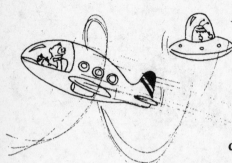

airborne

...5,687 airplanes take off
and land at Canada's
international airports
...181,079 passengers
are carried on these flights

...Vancouver International Airport handles 25,052 passengers and 521 flights
...Calgary International Airport handles 12,261 passengers and 276 flights
...Winnipeg International Airport handles 6,341 passengers and 156 flights
...Ottawa International Airport handles 7,222 passengers and 179 flights
...Montreal International Airport (Dorval) handles 17,687 passengers and 342 flights
...Halifax International Airport handles 6,576 passengers and 181 flights

on an average day...

...At Toronto's Pearson International Airport, the busiest in Canada,

959 flights take off and land

55,510 passengers use the terminals

25,000 meals are prepared by Cara Airlines Flight Services kitchens

Cara produces 40,000 rolls, 7,000 croissants, 5,000 muffins, 4,000 Danishes

600 people are sent to the Immigration Canada office

$273,973 worth of drugs is seized at the airport's passenger and cargo arrival depots

29,484 kilograms of freight are flown to Federal Express's main sorting facility in Memphis, Tennessee

60 pieces of luggage are left unclaimed or go missing

...The 10 busiest air routes within Canada are:

Montreal – Toronto	3,732 passengers
Ottawa – Toronto	2,162 passengers
Toronto – Vancouver	2,148 passengers
Calgary – Toronto	1,342 passengers
Calgary – Vancouver	1,164 passengers
Toronto – Winnipeg	1,101 passengers
Edmonton – Toronto	934 passengers
Edmonton – Vancouver	921 passengers
Calgary – Edmonton	910 passengers
Halifax – Toronto	899 passengers

on an average day...

...The 10 busiest Canadian/U.S. air routes are:

Toronto – New York	2,207 passengers
Montreal – New York	956 passengers
Toronto – Chicago	862 passengers
Toronto – Boston	727 passengers
Vancouver – Los Angeles	672 passengers
Toronto – Los Angeles	606 passengers
Toronto – Miami	503 passengers
Toronto – San Francisco	500 passengers
Montreal – Miami	487 passengers
Toronto – Tampa	429 passengers

...40,000 seats on Canadian aircraft are left unsold

...Canadian Airlines International handles 38,356 pieces of luggage
...1 piece of luggage goes missing or is stolen

...1 passenger is caught smoking in a Canadian aircraft lavatory

on an average day...

...Digger, a six-year-old beagle who works with his handler, Howard Clarke, an Agriculture Canada inspector at Pearson International Airport, uncovers 29 kilograms of undeclared meat, fruit, plants and dairy products

on track

...9,863 passengers ride VIA Rail trains

...It costs $898.80 for a one-way ticket aboard VIA Rail's luxury transcontinental service between Vancouver and Toronto on its refurbished 1950s vintage *Canadian*
...The same trip would cost $432.28 for a regular coach seat on an average VIA Rail train

...1 person is seriously hurt as the result of an accident involving a train

on an average day...

on the road

...11 millions cars are on Canadian roadways

...200,000 truckers use Canadian roads and highways

...356,305 cars and trucks use Canada's busiest stretch of highway, found in Metro Toronto on Highway 401, between Martingrove Road and Yonge Street

...86% of Canadians routinely use their seat belt
...Quebec has the highest average, with 93% of its residents using their seat belt

on an average day...

...Canadians buy 2,392 cars and 1,095 trucks

...Canadians buy:

782 General Motors cars
376 General Motors trucks
404 Ford cars
278 Ford trucks
303 Chrysler cars
266 Chrysler trucks
286 Hondas
209 Toyotas
94 Mazdas
92 Volkswagens
84 Nissans
60 Hyundais
23 Subarus
18 Suzukis
12 BMWs
11 Volvos
9 Mercedes-Benzes
2 Jaguars
2 Ladas

on an average day...

...110 Canadians will buy a car worth over $30,000, of which:

55 will be an Acura
7 will be a Lexus
4 will be an Audi
4 will be an Infiniti
2 will be a Jaguar

...The typical Canadian car costs $19.18 to operate and maintain

...7 million Canadians out of 9.4 million commuters go to work by car—in 87% of these cases, driving alone

...Runaway shopping carts do $273,973 worth of damage to cars parked in supermarket parking lots

on an average day...

...74 cars are towed away in Vancouver at an average cost of $15.50 each

...63 cars are towed away in Toronto at an average cost of $65 each

...42 cars in Edmonton are towed away at an average cost of $15 each

...5 cars are towed away in Halifax at an average cost of $40.66 each

...2 cars in Regina are towed away at an average cost of $28 each

...20,548 parking tickets are issued across Canada

...Getting a ticket while parked at an expired parking meter will cost:

$7.50 in Halifax
$35 in Montreal
$15 in Ottawa
$10 in Toronto
$20 in Calgary
$15 in Vancouver

on an average day...

...779 drivers are injured in motor vehicle accidents

Of those drivers injured,

   323 are injured in daytime accidents
   406 people are injured during night-time accidents
   50 people are injured in accidents occurring at 4:30 p.m.

...2 drivers fall asleep at the wheel and cause serious personal injury to themselves and others

public transportation

...1,258,175 passengers use the Toronto Transit Commission (TTC), the country's largest public transportation system

...The College/Carlton streetcar route in Toronto is the busiest surface public transportation route in Canada, carrying 62,000 riders

on an average day...

...The four major transportation systems for the disabled compare as follows:

	VANCOUVER HANDY DART	TORONTO WHEEL TRANS	HAMILTON DARTS	OTTAWA PARATRANSPO
Cost per ride to the company	$14.63	$32.70	$14.01	$21.50
Number of rides	2,602	3,510	1,173	1,758
Number of rides not accommodated	26	421	2	2
Total cost	$38,082	$114,795	$16,438	$37,808

...9 people are fined by the Toronto Transit Commission for smoking on its property
...2 people are fined for nuisance

CRIMINAL
ACTIVITIES

on an average day...

crime watch

...7,123 crimes are
   reported to
   police
...740 violent
   crimes are
   committed
...85 sexual
   assaults take place, 8 of them on men
...311 cars and trucks are stolen
...77 robberies occur, 20 involving firearms

...356 cases of fraud are reported
...$136,986 is rung up on stolen credit cards
...$8,219 is stolen in bank robberies
...203 cheque frauds take place
...106 forgeries occur

...4,275 property offences occur

on an average day...

...4,274 Canadians have something stolen

...2 people are murdered
...Based on murders per capita in Canadian cities, Regina is the murder capital of Canada; the safest place to live is St. John's, Newfoundland

...$21,095,890 from the federal government goes towards paying for police, courts, jails and the legal aid system across Canada

...$164,384 worth of bootleg merchandise is seized by Customs officers and police, most of it non-registered trademark T-shirts and music-related items

...$1,917,809 worth of jewellery and precious gems is sold on the Canadian black market

---

on an average day...

theft

...589 Canadian homes are broken into
...The average value of property stolen is $1,794, with $239 worth of damage during the robbery

Of the total break-ins,

in 118 of the cases, no property is stolen
312 break-ins occur between 6:00 a.m. and 6:00 p.m.
177 occur between midnight and 6:00 a.m.
118 of the robbers are age 12 to 17
471 break-ins are committed by males

...4 bank robberies take place
...The average take per holdup is $2,735
...The three provinces with the most robberies are Quebec, Ontario and British Columbia

on an average day...

...$6 million never makes it into cash registers owing to theft or careless paperwork

Of the total,

    $3 million is lost to customer shoplifting
    $2 million is lost to theft by employees
    $1 million is lost owing to poor tracking of goods and sales

...274 cars are stolen, worth $821,918

Of the total,

    205 of them are eventually returned to their owner
    208 are stolen by amateur thieves for joyrides
    38 of the stolen cars are used in robbery getaways or to transport illegal drugs
    19 are stripped down for parts
    104 are stolen off city streets
    55 are stolen off residential driveways
    49 are taken from shopping centre parking lots
    38 are stolen out of underground parking lots
    69 stolen are not locked
    55 of them have their keys left in the ignition
    5 are running at the time of the theft

on an average day...

...822 car stereo systems are stolen
...8 car stereos are returned to their owner

...22 bicycles are stolen in Metro Toronto, the bike-theft
   capital of North America

By comparison,

   15 bicycles are stolen in New York
   11 are stolen in Montreal
   4 are stolen in Washington, D.C.

...An unsuspecting passenger at Canada's largest airport,
   Pearson International, falls victim to an organized
   roaming band of well-dressed cosmopolitan thieves,
   who snatch an average of $2,740 a day

offensive driving

...662 traffic offences, as defined under the *Criminal
   Code*, occur

on an average day...

...Speeding ticket fines across Canada are as follows:

	Minimum	Maximum
Nova Scotia	$77.50	$77.50
Quebec	$15.00	no maximum
Ontario	$28.75	$297.75
Manitoba	$20.00	$363.00
Alberta	$29.00	$172.00
British Columbia	$75.00	$100.00

...696 drivers in Toronto receive a speeding ticket

...Drunk drivers kill 8 Canadians and leave 274 people seriously injured or permanently maimed

...309 people are charged with impaired driving; fewer than 1% of these charges lead to convictions

on an average day...

violence against women

...It is estimated that 240 sexual assaults on women by someone they know are not reported to the police

Of the total,

  180 of these attacks occur in the victim's home
  149 of these women are physically injured
  21 are severely beaten
  29 are threatened with a weapon
  168 are verbally threatened

...288 women are physically attacked by strangers

elder abuse

...268 people over the age of 65 experience some form of abuse, usually by someone close to them

on an average day...

behind bars

...27 women are sent to jail
...110 men are sent to jail

...It costs taxpayers $2,191,781 to maintain the federal prison system

...It costs taxpayers the following to house one inmate in jail overnight:

Newfoundland: $134
Prince Edward Island: $121
Nova Scotia: $120
Ontario: $116
British Columbia: $106
Yukon: $101
Northwest Territories: $96
Quebec: $91
Manitoba: $86
Alberta: $83
New Brunswick: $83
Saskatchewan: $74
NATIONAL AVERAGE: $101

on an average day...

...There are 2,021 prisoners serving life sentences in Canadian prisons

...19 inmates are given temporary passes

...68 applications are reviewed by the National Parole Board

gun power

...2,321 gun permits are issued
...4 people are killed by a firearm
...3 people commit suicide using a gun
...8 guns are lost or stolen

on an average day...

...2,688 Canadians register a restricted firearm

...8,219 women buy a gun

COMINGS AND GOINGS

on an average day...

immigration

...The federal government spends $27,945,205 on immigration

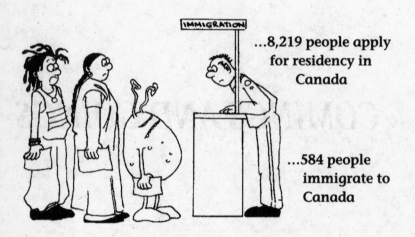

...8,219 people apply for residency in Canada

...584 people immigrate to Canada

...142 immigrants arrive from Europe
...37 immigrants arrive from Africa
...7 immigrants arrive from Australasia
...304 immigrants arrive from Asia
...70 immigrants arrive from North and Central America
...24 immigrants arrive from South America

on an average day...

...Immigrants to Canada settle in the following provinces:

78 in British Columbia
52 in Alberta
6 in Saskatchewan
18 in Manitoba
310 in Ontario
111 in Quebec
2 in New Brunswick
4 in Nova Scotia
1 in Prince Edward Island
2 in Newfoundland

...The top 10 countries of origin of Canada's immigrants are:

Hong Kong: 60
Poland: 42
China: 38
India: 35
Philippines: 33
Lebanon: 33
Vietnam: 24
United Kingdom: 20
El Salvador: 19
Sri Lanka: 19

on an average day...

...8,219 people are examined by border patrols before being allowed to enter Canada

...685 immigrants are interviewed, have security checks run on them and are medically examined before entering Canada

...1,918 temporary visas to students and short-term workers are issued

...411 immigrants seek sponsorship by a Canadian citizen before immigrating

...93 new immigrants take advantage of the federally supported language training programs

...Visas are issued for applicants coming to Canada from the following countries:

Asia and the Pacific Rim: 98
Western Europe: 63
United States: 36
Latin America and the Caribbean: 31
The Middle East: 26
Eastern Europe: 16
Africa: 5

on an average day...

the status of refugees

...100 refugees ask for
political asylum
in Canada

...The top 10
countries with
the most
accepted refugees are
the following:

Country	Accepted	Rejected
Sri Lanka	10	1
Somalia	8	1
Lebanon	4	1
Iran	4	1
El Salvador	3	1
China	1	4
Bulgaria	1	2
Pakistan	1	1
Romania	1	1

...12 refugees are deported from Canada
...1 of these refugees has a criminal record

on an average day...

becoming Canadian

...301 people from 170 countries are granted Canadian citizenship

Of the total,

39 are from Great Britain
18 are from Vietnam
15 are from Hong Kong
15 are from Poland
15 are from China
12 are from the Philippines
12 are from India
12 are from Portugal
9 are from Italy

Of the new Canadian citizens,

...53,900 reside in Ontario
...18,700 reside in Quebec
...16,500 reside in British Columbia

...13 applications for citizenship are turned down

on an average day...

Canadians on the move

...103 Canadians emigrate

...Interprovincial migration is as follows:

The Atlantic Provinces lose 17 citizens
Quebec loses 18 people
Ontario gains 61 new residents
Manitoba loses 16 people
Saskatchewan loses 32 citizens
Alberta loses 30 residents
British Columbia receives 52 people

...35 British Columbians move to Ontario
...70 Ontarians move to British Columbia

...10 people move to Kelowna, British Columbia, known
  fondly as Canada's Palm Springs
Of the total, 3 people move there from Ontario

on an average day...

...60 people in the private sector are transferred within Canada because of their job

...60 civil servants are transferred within Canada because of their job

...37 Canadians are transferred to jobs in the United States

EARNING OUR KEEP

on an average day...

the working Canadian

...Employed men spend 8 hours and 42 minutes doing paid work

...Employed women spend 7 hours and 30 minutes doing paid work

...1.7 million Canadians work more than 10 hours a day

...473,000 Canadians hold down two jobs

...The average Canadian woman earns $68
...The average Canadian man earns $101

on an average day...

...4.3 million Canadians spend their working day in front of a computer screen

...3.3 million Canadians carry out their day's business from their home

...$8,219,178 is spent on home office supplies, furniture and services

...25 million jobs listed in the classified ads go unfilled

...300,000 jobs go begging because no one is found with the skills to fill them

...1.5 million Canadians are unemployed

on an average day...

...959 Canadians take job training courses to retrain for new careers

...1.8 million employable physically disabled people are unemployed

...2,603 men apply for unemployment insurance
...2,432 women apply for unemployment insurance

...14,552 Canadians opt for early retirement
...255 Canadians who turn 65 are forced into mandatory retirement

...Canadians invest $46,575,342 in Registered Retirement Savings Plans

on an average day...

...Canada's largest pension plan, the Ontario Teachers' Pension Plan, grows by $12,602,739 in assets

...238 Canadians become members of labour unions
...Employees at 3 businesses go on strike or are locked out
...9,589 workdays are lost to major strikes and lockouts in Canada
...614 employees are on picket duty

...On average, the following professionals earn:

Physicians/surgeons: $312
Dentists: $259
Lawyers: $250
Accountants: $180
Engineers: $127
Architects: $127
Teachers/professors: $120

on an average day...

...Canada's richest resident, publishing baron Lord Thomson of Fleet, earns $628,560

...2 people are killed on the job
...1,607 people are injured
...Back injuries, the most common work-related ailment, cost $2,739,726 in compensation benefits

...Canada's largest office complex, First Canadian Place in Toronto, hosts a daytime population of 30,000 and...

uses 375,000 kilowatt-hours of electricity
consumes 1.6 million litres of water
burns 4,500 fluorescent lights

on an average day...

money, money, money

...4,693,717 circulating Canadian coins are struck by the Royal Canadian Mint

Of the total coins minted,

509,589 are loonies ($1 coins)

567 are 50-cent pieces

326,027 are quarters

542,466 are dimes

386,301 are nickels

2,928,767 are pennies

...2,284,932 new bank notes are issued

...The number of Canadian bank notes in circulation:

$2 bills: 201,466,000

$5 bills: 157,156,000

$10 bills 116,630,000

$20 bills: 396,840,000

$50 bills: 68,732,000

$100 bills: 76,770,000

$1,000 bills: 1,380,000

on an average day...

...The Royal Canadian Mint sells 80,088 grams of gold

...967 Maple Leaf gold coins are purchased, weighing 9,848 grams

...205 people tour the Royal Canadian Mint in Ottawa

...Canadians collectively hold $100 billion worth of Guaranteed Investment Certificates

...Canadians hold $11 billion worth of money market funds

...Canadians purchase $10,410,958 of U.S. stocks

on an average day...

...20 million cheques are cleared in the Toronto Clearing Exchange, with a total value of $33,333,333,000

...139,726 new credit cards are issued

...Canadians owe $30,136,986 to VISA and MasterCard

...$4,657,534 worth of VISA traveller's cheques are issued

...Canada's 6 national banks earn the following:

The Royal Bank earns $2,693,151
The Canadian Imperial Bank of Commerce earns $2,221,918
The Bank of Nova Scotia earns $1,734,247
The Bank of Montreal earns $1,630,137
The Toronto Dominion Bank earns $1,363,014
The National Bank of Canada earns $509,589

on an average day...

...Banks loose $10,959 to bank robbers and slippery-fingered employees

...4 Canadians file a registered complaint against their bank with the Federal Superintendent of Banking in Ottawa

MINDING OUR
BUSINESSES

on an average day...

taking care of business

...The top 10 most profitable public companies, listed on Canadian stock exchanges, earn the following:

BCE Inc.	$3,641,095
Bell Canada	$2,701,370
Royal Bank of Canada	$2,694,427
Canadian Imperial Bank of Commerce	$2,222,477
Seagram Ltd.	$1,991,781
Bank of Nova Scotia	$1,734,288
Bank of Montreal	$1,630,214
Northern Telecom	$1,410,685
Toronto Dominion Bank	$1,362,937
GW Utilities	$1,115,068

...Revenue garnered by Canada's top 10 private companies is as follows:

General Motors of Canada Ltd.	$52,887,419
Sun Life Assurance of Canada	$21,715,624
Chrysler Canada	$19,532,602

on an average day...

Manufacturer's Life Insurance	$18,556,416
Confederation Life Insurance	$18,317,750
IBM Canada	$17,298,630
Canada Life Assurance	$12,849,167
Imasco Enterprises	$12,493,980
Imasco Financial	$12,216,180
Canada Safeway	$11,889,279

...Stress costs Canadian businesses $32,876,712 in lost work time and absenteeism

...Fraud costs Canadian businesses $21,917,808

...Canadian businesses buy $16,438,356 worth of office supplies
...Grand & Toy is the leading supplier, with sales of $780,820

on an average day...

...207 bankruptcies occur

Of the total,

	PERSONAL	BUSINESS
Atlantic Provinces	9	3
Quebec	50	14
Ontario	72	10
Western Provinces	39	10

...63,288 business trips are taken
...50% of them are extended for pleasure time

command performances

...A 2-hour keynote speech or sales pitch would cost:

$133,320 if given by former prime minister Pierre Trudeau

$13,320 if given by former leader of the Ontario NDP Stephen Lewis

$6,666 if given by disgraced track star Angella Issajenko

$1,500 if given by a professional stand-up comedian

on an average day...

$666 if given by a poet at Toronto's Harbourfront
$500.40 if given by a BMW salesperson trying to sell a
car to a prospective buyer
$39.60 if given by a phone-sex raconteur

industrial strength

...If unpaid
housework were
considered an
industry, it
would be worth
$547,945,200, an
amount greater
than that of the
entire manufacturing industry in Canada
...Total time spent doing housework: 56,712,328 hours
...Total time spent doing paid work: 58,082,191 hours

...The textile and apparel industry is worth $38,356,164

on an average day...

...Canada's food service industry is worth $72,328,767

...The Canadian Chopstick Manufacturing Company Ltd., located in Fort Nelson, British Columbia, produces 4.5 million pairs of chopsticks

the power of advertising

...$27,671,232 is spent on advertising

...Canada's biggest spenders on advertising are the following:

The Thomson Group	$207,671
General Motors of Canada	$187,123
Government of Canada	$184,383
Procter & Gamble	$184,110
Sears Canada	$175,068
Molson Breweries of Canada	$144,384

on an average day...

Paramount Communications	$122,466
Unilever Canada Ltd.	$120,000
Cineplex Odeon Corporation	$117,534
John Labatt Ltd.	$117,534
Ontario Government	$98,356
Toyota Canada	$77,808
Ford of Canada Ltd.	$77,260
Pepsico Inc.	$72,603
Coca-Cola Ltd.	$53,425
Air Canada	$46,575

...$2,534,247 is spent on advertising sporting events in Canada

...Wayne Gretzky earns $13,699 in endorsements

...Canadian magazines sell 82 pages of advertising, taking in $919,726 worth of revenue

on an average day...

...Canadian Tire distributes a million advertising circulars

...64,109,589 coupons are distributed
...679,452 are redeemed

...41 complaints of misleading advertising are received
   by Consumer and Corporate Affairs Canada
...Fines for false or misleading advertising total $2,487

on an average day...

down on the farm

...890,500 Canadians work on Canada's 260,745 farms

Of the total farms in Canada,

    59,262 raise cattle
    58,595 grow small grains
    46,857 grow wheat
    34,186 raise dairy cattle
    14,449 are miscellaneous specialties
    12,026 are hog farms
    10,377 grow fruits and vegetables
    8,850 practice mixed farming
    5,918 grow field crops
    5,577 raise mixed livestock
    4,648 are poultry farms

...Canadian farmers sell $57,479,863 worth of products

on an average day...

...The top yielding commodity for each province is:

Newfoundland	poultry	$34,732
Prince Edward Island	potatoes	$312,539
Nova Scotia	dairy products	$238,002
New Brunswick	potatoes	$214,348
Quebec	dairy products	$3,198,584
Ontario	dairy products	$2,932,285
Manitoba	wheat	$1,366,736
Saskatchewan	wheat	$3,816,151
Alberta	cattle	$4,245,682
British Columbia	dairy products	$686,962

...20,179,000 litres of milk are produced

...Maple Lodge Farms, Canada's largest chicken producer, processes 180,000 to 230,000 birds

...1,148,282 chickens, turkeys and ducks are slaughtered
...42,679 pigs are slaughtered
...7,861 cattle are slaughtered
...1,105 calves are slaughtered
...437 lambs are slaughtered

on an average day...

cash cows

...A Hong Kong pharmaceutical company offers Canadian farmers $13.20 a gram for whole cattle gallstones for use in Chinese medicine (gold is worth about $11.80 a gram)

...A 1,140 kilogram Canadian Holstein bull named Madawaska Aerostar (also known as "The Most Popular Bull in the World, the Don Juan of the Animal Kingdom") produces 357 tubes of semen, which is collected three times a day after he is teased by a steer (the semen is sold in thin plastic tubes for $40 each)

on an average day...

bumper crops

...The 10 most "fruitful" crops grown on Canadian farms are:

Apples: $468,227 worth
Strawberries: $131,016 worth
Blueberries: $107,772 worth
Raspberries: $93,614 worth
Grapes: $82,082 worth
Peaches: $73,449 worth
Cranberries: $41,074 worth
Pears: $25,112 worth
Sweet cherries: $17,345 worth
Sour cherries: $12,507 worth

...Canadian orchards produce 1,332,000 kilograms of apples
...We import 383,562 kilograms of apples from the United States

on an average day...

...The 10 most valuable veggies grown on Canadian farms are:

Potatoes: $1,238,378 worth
Mushrooms: $435,515 worth
Tomatoes: $285,205 worth
Corn: $179,748 worth
Carrots: $121,619 worth
Cabbages: $92,573 worth
Onions: $84,923 worth
Peas: $77,022 worth
Cauliflowers: $72,726 worth
Lettuce: $69,570 worth

just milling around

...Canadian farmers produce 71,000 tonnes of wheat; 6,700 tonnes are milled into flour

on an average day...

how sweet it is

...Canadian bees produce 110,867 kilograms of honey, 6% of the world's supply

Of the total amount of Canadian honey,

...27,717 kilograms are produced by Alberta bees

...Canadian farmers grow 2,623,848 kilograms of sugar beets

...Canadian maple trees provide 723,000 kilolitres of maple syrup

on an average day...

outstanding in their field

...John Bragg of Nova Scotia grows, harvests, freezes and sells more wild blueberries than anyone anywhere— 33,699 kilograms worth $73,973

...His crop accounts for 30% of the North American total

...Chai-Na-Ta Ginseng Products Ltd. of Langley, British Columbia, the largest grower of ginseng in North America, sells $20,274 worth of the aromatic root, which is used for medicine, especially in China

...3,308 kilograms of wild rice are produced by farms in Ontario, Manitoba, Saskatchewan and Prince Edward Island

on an average day...

the tractor factor

...41 Canadians buy a farm tractor

pharmaceuticals

...Canada's pharmaceutical companies take in $11,780,821 in sales

...Sales of generic medications total $931,507

...3 million Aspirin tablets are produced

...Apotex Inc., the largest Canadian-owned pharmaceutical company, produces a million headache pills— no-name acetaminophen tablets

on an average day...

...Sandoz Canada's Whitby plant produces all the Neo Citran cold medication sold in North America and Europe—they make 452,055 individual pouches

...Connaught Laboratories Ltd. of Toronto distributes 273,973 doses of its vaccines around the world
...3,562 doses of the DPT vaccine (diphtheria, pertussis and tetanus) are sent to Taiwan

...Canadian pharmaceutical companies spend $1,060,274 on research and development of new products

on an average day...

software

...Canadian software manufacturers sell $6,849,315 worth of original programs

...Canadian computer software manufacturers lose $547,946 in revenue owing to illegal copying of their original software by individuals and businesses

EARTH WATCH

on an average day...

environmental update

...The federal government's Green Plan will cost taxpayers $9,726,027 a day for the next 20 years

...8,219 tonnes of hazardous waste are released into the Canadian environment. (There are four major categories of hazardous waste: by-products of industrial manufacturing; discarded consumer products; residues accidentally spilled in storage or transportation; discarded products and residues from laboratories and institutions.)

not-so-fresh air

...278,319 tonnes of chlorofluorocarbons (CFCs) and halons are released into our atmosphere

on an average day...

...12,329 kilograms of herbicides containing dioxins are used in the Canadian prairies to kill broadleaf weeds

...8,219 kilograms of herbacides are used as wood preservatives

...The federal government spends $68,493 on the 20-year acid rain program initiated in 1985

...According to a Ministry of the Environment survey of six North American cities of similar size, Vancouver had the cleanest air, followed by Montreal, Atlanta, Boston, Chicago and, lastly, Toronto

water crisis

...Canadians purchase $547,945 worth of bottled water

...$1,780,822 is spent on water purification systems for the home or cottage

on an average day...

...800 tonnes of solid waste materials are dumped into our waterways

...107 tonnes of chlorine are dumped into our waterways

...Canadians use 2,739,726 litres of lubricating oil and dispose of 1,164,383 litres

Of this amount,

821,918 litres end up in our waterways, 7 times the amount of oil that the *Exxon Valdez* spilled off the coast of Alaska

The remaining 342,465 litres of the dumped oil is burned as fuel

...1,369,863 litres of untreated sewage flow into the St. Lawrence River

on an average day...

...The 230,000 residents of Victoria, British Columbia, send 55 million litres of human excrement, toxic waste and other hazardous liquid through a long pipe that stretches 1,100 metres out into the Strait of Juan de Fuca

...Canadians are the second largest per capita users of water in the world (after the United States): we use 360 litres for every man, woman and child

Of this total,

142 litres of water are used to flush the toilet
107 litres are used for bathing
55 litres are used for laundry
37 litres are used for dishes
19 litres are used for cooking and drinking

...Vancouver residents are, statistically speaking, water hogs, using 1,000 litres per person—this is 25% more than their U.S. neighbours in Seattle, Washington, use

on an average day...

reduce, refuse and recycle

...Canadians dispose of 1.8 kilograms of garbage per person

...5,479,452 disposable diapers are thrown out
...3,561,644 feminine pads and tampons are thrown into the garbage

...A kilogram of table scraps is thrown out by a family of four

...7.8 million Canadians recycle, no matter how much effort it takes
...15.6 million Canadians recycle bottles, cans and newspapers
...2.6 million do not recycle anything

on an average day...

...159 tonnes of glass collected from blue boxes are recycled by Consumers Glass
Of the total, 95 tonnes are from liquor and wine bottles

...Residents of British Columbia throw out 3,835,616 bottles and cans, of which 2,301,370 end up in landfill or litter, despite the municipal blue box program

...200 dirty medical syringes wash ashore on Toronto's Sunnyside Beach

group action

...219 Canadians become members of Greenpeace

on an average day...

...Greenpeace Canada raises $32,877 from donations and membership fees

...68 Canadians become supporters of Pollution Probe
...Pollution Probe raises $3,014 from individual donations and membership fees
...Pollution Probe receives 45 telephone calls and 10 letters from the general public

weather report

...221,917,800 tonnes of hail, rain and/or snow fall on Canada

...Estevan, Saskatchewan, receives the most sunlight of any place in Canada—about 7 hours

on an average day...

...Prince Rupert, British Columbia, receives the least sunlight of any place in Canada—about 3 hours

...Salt damage to Canadian roads costs taxpayers $657,534

fire alarm

...Canadian firefighters are called to 184 fires

...Of the fires reported,

25 are caused by arson
3 are caused by careless smoking
4 are caused by children playing with matches

on an average day...

...The value of property lost due to fire is $2,619,700

...Canada's busiest firehall is Station 7 in Toronto at Parliament and Gerrard streets
...Fire trucks from this station make 27 runs and the aerial truck is called out on 8 runs

...31 forest fires occur

...18,184 hectares of woodland are destroyed by fire

energy, mines and resources

...Canada produces 263,334,240 cubic metres of natural gas valued at $14,778,082

on an average day...

...Canada produces 193,225 tonnes of coal valued at $4,775,342

...Canada produces 1,276,622 megawatt-hours of electricity

...Canadian nuclear power plants generate 382,378 megawatt-hours of electrical power

...Oil production in Canada is worth $32,202,739

...Canada produces 1,674,000 barrels of oil

...Canada uses 1,454,000 barrels of oil

...Canada's per capita energy use is the world's highest, at 24 kilograms of oil per person

on an average day...

...Canada's most valuable mined resources are:

Oil: $37,895,342
Natural gas: $15,335,710
Copper: $6,834,520
Zinc: $6,786,301
Gold: $6,515,890
Nickel: $5,545,205
Coal: $5,126,027
Iron Ore: $3,595,068

...Mineral production in Canada is as follows:

Cement: 30,827 tonnes
Coal: 187,534 tonnes
Copper: 2,135,797 kilograms
Gold: 452,030 grams
Iron ore: 99,843 tonnes
Nickel: 538,646 kilograms
Potash: 19,219 tonnes
Sand and gravel: 685,123 tonnes
Uranium: 25,912 kilograms
Zinc: 3,521,750 kilograms

on an average day...

TIMBER!!!!!!!!!!!!!!!!!!!!!!!!!!!

...The forest products sector, Canada's largest industry, is worth $87,397,260

...It employs 250,000 Canadians directly and 750,000 indirectly

...1,917,808 trees are cut down

...2,191,781 trees are planted

...The harvesting and replanting of trees in our provinces is as follows:

	HECTARES OF TREES HARVESTED	HECTARES OF TREES REPLANTED
British Columbia	598	122
Alberta	124	238
Saskatchewan	59	15
Manitoba	33	17
Ontario	650	222
Quebec	937	274
New Brunswick	247	51
Nova Scotia	103	31
Prince Edward Island	6.5	2.4
Newfoundland	60	73

on an average day...

...Canada produces 27,397 tonnes of newsprint, of which only 3,288 tonnes remain in Canada—the rest is exported to the United States

...The Canadian paper industry exports $39,178,082 worth of newsprint and other types of paper
...$23,506,849 worth of these products is exported to the United States

...Canada exports $9,589,041 worth of forest products to Europe

...Canadians use 23,600 tonnes of paper

...Canadians recycle 5,205 tonnes of paper

on an average day...

...Canadians use 5,205 tonnes of recycled paper

...109,589 trees are cut down in order to provide pulp and paper for Canada's book publishing industry

...Toronto's City Hall uses 356,164 sheets of paper, the equivalent of 48 trees

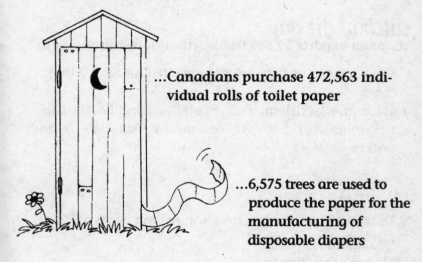

...Canadians purchase 472,563 individual rolls of toilet paper

...6,575 trees are used to produce the paper for the manufacturing of disposable diapers

on an average day...

...Mik-O-Tec Investments Inc., owned by Michael Lim of Richmond, British Columbia, sells 2,732 of his biodegradable golf tees to Canadian proshops. He sells 5,464 of the tees to the western United States and 1,639 of them to Japan. The tees dissolve within 24-36 hours after they come into contact with water. Each of the tees lasts for one and a half holes.

...To make regular wooden golf tees, 115 birch trees must be cut

catch of the day

...3,411 tonnes of fish are caught off Canada's Atlantic coast
...618 tonnes of fish are caught off Canada's Pacific coast
...125 tonnes of fish are caught in Canada's inland waters

...The top 12 catches by Canadian fishing boats are:

1,333 tonnes of cod
556 tonnes of herring
207 tonnes of salmon
123 tonnes of haddock

on an average day...

120 tonnes of crab
104 tonnes of lobster
44 tonnes of clams
44 tonnes of shrimp
30 tonnes of halibut
14 tonnes of oysters
3 tonnes of eel
1 tonne of tuna

...Canada imports 484 tonnes of fish
...Canada exports 1,610 tonnes of fish

...60 tonnes of Pacific pink salmon is canned
...35 tonnes of Pacific red sockeye salmon is canned

trappings

...The fur industry in Canada is worth $205,479

Of the total,

...$93,151 is from wildlife pelts, and the remaining $112,328 is from ranch-raised animals

on an average day...

Of the wildlife pelts,

...half the value is from marten ($45,753) followed by beaver ($16,986)

Of the ranch-raised pelts,

...$95,890 is from mink and the remainder from fox

...178 baby harp seals are slaughtered for their pelts

animal research and testing

...The following number of animals are used for research, testing or teaching:

2,219 mice
1,096 rats
767 fish
740 fowl
110 guinea pigs
96 rabbits
55 dogs
27 cats
27 monkeys

BUY, SELL, TRADE

on an average day...

imports/exports

...Canada imports $372,389,000 worth of goods

...Canada exports $405,945,000 worth of goods

...The top 12 imports into Canada are:

Automotive parts, except engines	$33,424,657
Cars	$32,054,794
Computers	$18,082,191
Crude petroleum	$12,328,767
Telecommunications equipment	$10,958,904
Special transactions, trade	$10,410,958
Semi-conductors	$9,041,099
Trucks	$7,671,233
Motor vehicle engines	$7,397,260
Organic chemicals	$5,479,452
Equipment, tools	$5,205,479
Aircraft	$4,383,562

on an average day...

trading partners

...The top 10 countries Canada imports goods from:

COUNTRY	TOTAL VALUE
United States	$240,556,160
Japan	$26,073,970
United Kingdom	$13,260,270
Germany	$10,498,630
South Korea	$6,169,860
Taiwan	$5,778,080
Italy	$5,350,680
Mexico	$4,739,720
China	$3,813,700
Hong Kong	$2,901,370

...The top 10 countries we export goods to:

COUNTRY	TOTAL VALUE
United States	$304,663,000
Japan	$22,506,850
United Kingdom	$9,619,180
Germany	$6,301,370
China	$4,531,500
South Korea	$4,282,190
Netherlands	$4,150,680
France	$3,567,120
Belgium	$3,389,040
Italy	$3,213,700

on an average day...

...Canada's 6 most important imports from the United States, our number-one trading partner, are:

Motor vehicle parts	$39,997,260
Chemicals	$28,706,849
Automobiles	$22,243,853
Food	$18,093,150
Computers	$11,553,424
Telecommunications equipment	$10,602,739

...Canada's 6 most important exports to the United States are:

Wood and paper	$75,638,356
Metal ores and alloys	$49,476,712
Automobiles	$43,210,958
Motor vehicle parts	$27,032,876
Chemicals	$24,641,095
Trucks	$19,682,191

...Canada does $16,301 worth of business with Indiana, our biggest trading partner of the 50 states

on an average day...

...Japan buys $22,191,780 worth of Canadian goods

...Japan invests $13,698,630 in Canada
...Japanese companies in Canada employ 24,000 people
...Canada invests $1,095,890 in Japan
...1,315 business trips are made by the Japanese to Canada
...175 business trips by Canadians are made to Japan

...Canada's most important imports from Mexico are:

Automotive parts (except engines)	$1,865,479
Passenger cars	$1,845,205
Vehicle engines	$560,822
Computers:	$352,603
Crude petroleum	$247,397

...Canada's most important exports to Mexico are:

Automotive parts (except engines)	$330,411
Newsprint	$108,219

on an average day...

Steel	$103,836
Trucks and chassis	$76,164
Wheat	$68,493

...Canada's most important imports from South Africa are:

Ferrochromium for steel making	$41,644
Platinum for aerospace parts	$36,712
Rhodium for electrical wire	$34,247
Aluminium alloys	$21,370
Ferromanganese for steel making	$20,822

...Canada's most important exports to South Africa are:

Wheat	$232,877
Sulphur	$61,096
Nickel	$20,274
Potassium chloride	$16,986
Ash residue and copper	$8,767

on an average day...

specialty trade

...Canada imports 4,110 ceiling fans

...Sabian Cymbals of Meductic, New Brunswick, sells 548 cymbals worth $27,397

...493 of the cymbals are shipped to more than 80 countries around the world

...$109,589 worth of Canadian beef is sold to Japan

...The Northwest Territories imports 370 kilograms of soapstone from British Columbia and Virginia

on an average day...

...1,041 Canadian-made men's wool suits, valued at $136,986, are exported to the United States

...4,109,589 Ontario worms are exported to the United States and Europe, giving Canada the distinction of being the worm capital of the world

what's in store?

...$176,712,320 is spent in Canada's 3,376 shopping malls

...5,300,679 paper bags are shipped to Canadian retailers

...Dave Nichol, head of product development for Loblaws Companies Ltd., introduces a new President's Choice product

on an average day...

...The Canadian discount industry makes $24,657,534 in sales

...K Mart earns $3,013,699 from its Canadian stores

...Ed Mirvish's Honest Ed's bargain store in Toronto does $178,082 worth of business

...Price Club Canada attracts 3,000 shoppers, who spend $3,287,671

...Consumers Distributing distributes 13,699 catalogues to Canadian households, and takes in $1,917,808 worth of sales

...109,589 Canadians receive a catalogue from Sears

...$6,027,397 is spent by Canadians on products from one of Canada's 600 catalogue firms

on an average day...

if the shoe fits...

...91,688 pairs of shoes are manufactured in Canada
Of these,

  8,518 pairs are for men and boys
  30,414 pairs are for women and girls
  2,400 pairs are for children and infants
  9,830 pairs are work and utility footwear
  15,205 pairs are slippers
  9,866 pairs are athletic footwear
  8,351 pairs are waterproof, rubber or plastic footwear

...215,274 pairs of shoes are imported into Canada
Of these,

  20,482 pairs are for men and boys
  52,055 pairs are for women and girls
  10,088 pairs are for children and infants
  575 pairs are work and utility footwear

on an average day...

15,110 pairs are slippers
60,342 pairs are athletic footwear
12,192 pairs are waterproof, rubber and plastic footwear

...Revenues from the retail sale of shoes in Canada are $6,216,268

Of the total,

$4,621,627 worth of shoes is sold by independent shoe stores and chains
$1,594,641 worth of shoes is sold by department stores

...$219,178 worth of footwear is imported from Italy

...Canadians buy $19,178 worth of Hush Puppies shoes

...Bi-Way Stores sell 16,438 pairs of shoes

on an average day...

fashion statement

...Canada imports **$13,698,630 worth of clothing and textiles**

...**274 Tilley Endurables hats are sold**

...**Women buy $32,876,712 worth of clothing**

...Of the **$2,232,877 worth of diamond jewellery purchased for women, $312,603 (14%) of it is bought by women for themselves**

on an average day...

...John Ivanauskas of Applause Applause repairs the 10 mannequins that arrive at his shop suffering from broken backs, missing fingers, sometimes severed heads

high tech

...2,740 personal computers are purchased, half of which are clones

Of the total,

    1,511 are purchased by small businesses
    652 are purchased by individuals
    577 are purchased by schools and government

...822 personal computers are purchased

...148 people buy a laptop computer

...147 Canadians buy a fax machine

GOVERNMENT
AND POLITICS

on an average day...

the feds

...It costs taxpayers $13,699 to cover the cost of the satellite required to beam the federal parliamentary proceedings across Canada on the Parliamentary Channel

...Canada's national debt increases by $82,080,000

...$647,068 worth of taxpayers' money is needed to run the House of Commons

...MPs spend $34,712 travelling between Ottawa and their ridings

...The parliamentary dining room loses $8,466 owing to the highly subsidized prices

...$16 is spent on the salary of a part-time aerobics instructor for the Senators

...$95 is spent on the salary of a full-time picture framer for the Senators

on an average day...

...It costs Canadian taxpayers $273,973 to cover the cost of 28,600 vehicles owned by government departments and agencies

...Canadian taxpayers dole out $13,425 to pay for Prime Minister Brian Mulroney's 60 personal RCMP bodyguards

...It costs $50.68 to fire the noonday cannon on Parliament Hill

...Drug testing of federal government employees costs $273,972
...2,082 urine samples are collected from workers covered by this mandatory program at a cost of $40 per sample, a total cost to taxpayers of $83,280

on an average day...

...The federal Conservatives ring up $726,027 worth of transactions on their government-issued American Express and/or MasterCards

...It costs $681 for capital and operating costs at 24 Sussex Drive, the prime minister's residence
...It costs $195 to keep Stornoway, the residence of the Leader of the Official Opposition

...It costs Canadian taxpayers $8,767 to operate Rideau Hall, the official residence of the Governor General of Canada

...96 people are invited to Rideau Hall

...Canada spends $35,068,493 on national defence

on an average day...

...The Canadian troops living on the "Canada Dry" base during the Gulf War consumed:

250 loaves of bread
114 kilograms of meat
1,000 eggs
1,600 individual packets of peanut butter
The laundry service washed 500 loads of laundry, and the cooks prepared 310 meals three times a day, plus 125 extra for guests

...Federal Royal Commissions cost taxpayers $273,973

...Canada's Unemployment Insurance Fund pays out $53,888,889 to the unemployed

...11,233 Family Allowance cheques are mailed out

on an average day...

...Canada's underground economy costs the government
$246,575,340

the GST

...The GST adds $49,315,068 to the federal government
coffers

...6,000 calls are
received by the GST
consumer
information office

...The federal government collects $54,795 of GST on
feminine sanitary products, a market worth $791,780

on an average day...

the price of politics

...The number of contributors to the federal political parties are:

262 to the New Democratic Party
125 to the Reform Party
95 to the Conservatives
83 to the Liberals
5 to the Confederation of Regions Western Party
2 to the Green Party
2 to the Christian Heritage Party
1 to the Communist Party
1 to the Libertarian Party

...The following political donations are made:

Jean Chrétien gives $6.49 to the Liberal Party
Audrey McLaughlin gives $5.95 to the NDP
Preston Manning gives $4.11 to the Reform Party
Brian Mulroney gives $3.15 to the Conservative Party

on an average day...

...Canada's most generous individual donation to a federal party is from Irene Dyck of Calgary, Alberta, who gives $347 to the New Democratic Party

...Canadian banks make the following political donations:

Toronto Dominion Bank: $124 to the Conservatives and Liberals

Bank of Montreal: $120 to the Conservatives and Liberals

Canadian Imperial Bank of Commerce: $112 to the Conservatives and $175 to the Liberals

Bank of Nova Scotia: $112 to the Conservatives and Liberals

National Bank of Canada: $68.70 to the Conservatives and Liberals

...The federal Conservative Party receives $30,137 in political donations

...The federal Liberal Party receives $32,877 in political donations

...The federal New Democratic Party receives $42,192 in political donations

on an average day...

dear sir

...Prime Minister Brian Mulroney receives 274 letters

...The Reform Party receives 1,400 pieces of mail at its headquarters in Calgary, Alberta

OPINION POLLS

on an average day...

the inside scoop

...When Canadians are asked which one of the following
options concerning the free trade agreement between
Canada and the United States they prefer...

...61% would like to see changes made to the agreement

...27% said they wanted it terminated

...7% have no opinion

...4% say that the agreement should be left as is

(Percentages do not add up to 100 owing to rounding off.)

on an average day...

...When Canadians are asked whether they think Brian Mulroney, Jean Chrétien, Audrey McLaughlin, Preston Manning and Lucien Bouchard care about the average Canadian, they reply:

	Yes	No	Don't Know
Mulroney	21%	71%	9%
Chrétien	41%	37%	22%
McLaughlin	48%	17%	35%
Manning	24%	23%	53%
Bouchard	22%	32%	47%

...When Canadians are asked whether they think Brian Mulroney, Jean Chrétien, Audrey McLaughlin, Preston Manning and Lucien Bouchard are strong and decisive leaders, they reply:

	Yes	No	Don't Know
Mulroney	24%	68%	8%
Chrétien	38%	42%	20%
McLaughlin	28%	32%	40%
Manning	21%	22%	57%
Bouchard	25%	28%	47%

on an average day...

...When Candians are asked whether Brian Mulroney is a prime minister they are proud of,

16% say yes
76% say no
8% say they don't know

...When Canadians are asked whether Jean Chrétien, Audrey McLaughlin or Preston Manning is a leader that they would be proud to have as prime minister, they reply:

	YES	NO	DON'T KNOW
Chrétien	29%	52%	19%
McLaughlin	26%	37%	37%
Manning	13%	32%	55%

...When Canadians are asked whether they think Brian Mulroney, Jean Chrétien, Audrey McLaughlin, Preston Manning and Lucien Bouchard are honest and trustworthy, they reply:

	YES	NO	DON'T KNOW
Mulroney	20%	66%	14%
Chrétien	40%	34%	26%
McLaughlin	45%	15%	40%

on an average day...

	Yes	No	Don't Know
Manning	22%	20%	58%
Bouchard	19%	29%	52%

...When Canadians are asked whether Canada should continue to have a monarch as its head of state or discontinue ties with the monarchy, they reply:

	Continue	Discontinue	No Opinion
Atlantic Provinces	58%	29%	13%
Quebec	22%	66%	12%
Ontario	55%	38%	7%
Prairie Provinces	52%	41%	7%
British Columbia	53%	40%	7%

...When Canadians are asked whether they favour or oppose permanently moving Canada Day to the closest Monday on or before July 1st, so it will always be part of a long holiday weekend,

71% are in favour
21% oppose
8% have no opinion

on an average day...

...When Canadians are asked whether Sunday shopping should be allowed,

67% say yes
8% say yes under special circumstances
23% say no
2% have no opinion

The regional breakdown is as follows:

	YES	YES UNDER SPECIAL CIRCUMSTANCES	NO	NO OPINION
Atlantic Provinces	58%	9%	32%	1%
Quebec	65%	16%	19%	0%
Ontario	68%	6%	22%	4%
Prairie Provinces	62%	5%	32%	2%
British Columbia	79%	3%	16%	2%
Toronto	75%	1%	21%	3%
Montreal	76%	7%	17%	0%

WHICH DO YOU PREFER: CHUNKY OR SMOOTH?

on an average day...

...When Canadians are asked if they favour or oppose marriages between people of the same sex:

24% are in favour
61% oppose
15% have no opinion

The regional breakdown is as follows:

	Favour	Oppose	No Opinion
Atlantic Provinces	19%	65%	16%
Quebec	33%	51%	16%
Ontario	23%	65%	13%
Prairie Provinces	20%	65%	15%
British Columbia	23%	65%	12%

would you believe?

...When asked,

7,540,000 Canadians believe in the Devil or Antichrist
3,640,000 believe in the Loch Ness Monster
2,860,000 believe in witches
780,000 believe in werewolves and vampires

on an average day...

...When asked, 1,820,000 Canadians say they believe Elvis is still alive

on the outside looking in

...The percentage of people in each country who believe Canadian aboriginals are poorly treated:

Australia: 46%
France: 56%
Germany: 68%
Hong Kong: 56%
India: 51%
Italy: 43%
Japan: 53%
Mexico: 46%
Commonwealth of Independent States: 20%
Singapore: 41%
South Korea: 61%
Spain: 49%
Taiwan: 39%
United Kingdom: 66%
United States: 47%

on an average day...

...The percentage of people in each country who agree that Canada follows the U.S. lead on foreign policy:

Australia: 39%
France: 39%
Germany: 51%
Hong Kong: 54%
India: 53%
Italy: 54%
Japan: 63%
Mexico: 61%
Commonwealth of Independent States: 36%
Singapore: 41%
South Korea: 40%
Spain: 58%
Taiwan: 24%
United Kingdom: 35%
United States: 48%

...The reaction in each country to the question, "How would you react to news of Quebec leaving Canada?" is as follows:

	HAPPY	SAD	UNMOVED
Australia	5%	45%	46%
France	29%	23%	46%

on an average day...

	HAPPY	SAD	UNMOVED
Germany	8%	46%	45%
Hong Kong	5%	9%	87%
India	5%	31%	45%
Italy	22%	23%	52%
Japan	9%	15%	49%
Mexico	7%	20%	71%
Commonwealth of Independent States	7%	44%	42%
Singapore	8%	26%	64%
South Korea	29%	9%	19%
Spain	10%	37%	53%
Taiwan	6%	15%	59%
United Kingdom	7%	45%	48%
United States	5%	42%	47%

(Percentages do not add up to 100 owing to non-responses.)

Sources

For the purposes of generating some daily statistics, the following information, available from Statistics Canada 1991 has been used: population of Canada: 26 million*; number of households in Canada: 10 million; number of seniors age 65 and over: 2.86 million; number of teenagers: 3.12 million; number of children age 5 and under: 1.9 million; number of people that live alone: 2.3 million.

*Statistics Canada's new figure (as of July 1992) for the population of Canada is 27 million. The impact of this population increase on *daily* figures is of no consequence.

HOW CANADIANS SPEND AN AVERAGE DAY
where time goes
p. 4, Canadian Global Almanac, 1992; p. 5, Canadian Global Almanac, 1992; p. 6, General Social Survey, Analysis Series, Statistics Canada, Catalogue 11-612E, No. 4; p. 7, General Social Survey, Analysis Series, Statistics Canada, Catalogue 11-612E, No. 4; p. 8, General Social Survey, Analysis Series, Statistics Canada, Catalogue 11-612E, No. 4; p. 9, General Social Survey, Analysis Series, Statistics Canada, Catalogue 11-612E, No. 4; p. 9, Medical Post, August 21/90

special days
p. 9, Hallmark Cards (birthday card); p. 9, Toronto Star, December 17/91; p. 10, Toronto Star, February 10/91; p. 10, Globe and Mail, May 2/92

on an average summer day
p. 10, Toronto Star, June 27/91

on an average St. Patrick's Day
p. 11, Financial Post Magazine, March 1991

on an average Valentine's Day
p. 11, Toronto Star, February 14/91

here comes the bride
p. 12, Wedding Council of Ontario, Statistics Canada, Toronto Star, February 20/92, Canadian Hotel and Restaurant, February 1992; p. 12, Toronto Star, June 7/91; p. 12, Globe and Mail, August 19/91

keeping the faith
p. 13, Gallup Canada, Toronto Star, June 6/92; p. 13, Toronto Star, April 19/92

DAILY DIVERSIONS

between the covers

p. 15, Toronto Star, November 22/91; p. 15, Maclean's, July 20/92; p. 15, Report on Business Magazine, January 1991, Statistics Canada; p. 15, Canadian Global Almanac, 1992; p. 16, Quill & Quire, May 1992; p. 16, Metro Toronto Reference Library, 1992, Toronto Star, September 11/90; p. 16, Globe and Mail, June 9/91; p. 16, Toronto Star, July 12/91; p. 16, Report on Business Magazine, December 31/91; p. 17, Toronto Star, April 8/91; p. 17, Globe and Mail, August 25/90; p. 17, Toronto Star, July 27/91; p. 17, Canadian Bible Society, 1991; p. 17, Canada Year Book, 1990

the fourth estate

p. 18, Newspaper Audience Databank, 1991, Toronto Star, October 5/91; p. 18-19, Audit Bureau of Circulations, FAS-FAX Report; p. 19, Toronto Star, March 6/92; p. 19, Goodlife, May 1991

keeping tabs on the tabloids

p. 20, Toronto Star, September 1/91

the glossies

p. 20-21, Audit Bureau of Circulations, 1991; p. 21, Canada 125, A supplement to the Globe and Mail, April 17/92

comic relief

p. 21, Report on Business Magazine, June 1991

TV times

p. 22, Consumer Electronics Marketers of Canada Report, Toronto Star, March 26/91; p. 22, Toronto Star, June 16/91, Federal Ministry of Employment Discussion Paper, October 1991, The Children's Broadcast Institute, Toronto Star, May 30/91; p. 22, General Social Survey, Analysis Series, Statistics Canada, Catalogue 11-612E, No. 4; p. 23, Toronto Star, April 20/91; p. 23, Toronto Life, June 1992; p. 23, Toronto Star, May 16/90; p. 23, Canadian Cable Television Association, Toronto Star, July 1/90; p. 23, Canada Year Book, 1990

live theatre

p. 24, Globe and Mail, May 23/92

Phantom unmasked

p. 24-25, Toronto Star, September 8/90, Toronto Star, April 7/91

at the movies

p. 25, Globe and Mail, May 9/92

private screenings

p. 25, Consumer Electronic Marketers of Canada Report, Toronto Star, March 26/91;
p. 25, Consumer Electronics Marketers of Canada Report, Toronto Star, June 11/90;
p. 26, Toronto Star, October 28/90, Toronto Star, March 26/91; p. 26, Globe and Mail, April

14/91, Starweek Magazine, March 7-12/92, Toronto Star, November 30/91, Toronto Star, December 24/91; p. 26, Toronto Star, June 4/91; p. 26, Canada Year Book, 1990

music to the ears
p. 27, Toronto Star, November 30/91, Toronto Magazine, January/February 1991, Toronto Star, March 11/92; p. 27, Toronto Star, March 2/91; p. 27, Canada Year Book, 1990

aiding the arts
p. 28, Maclean's, July 20/92

it's worth a gamble
p. 28, Globe and Mail, May 9/92; p. 28, Canadian Business, August 1990; p. 29, Ontario Lottery Report 1990-1991; p. 29, Toronto Star, March 29/92; p. 29, Maclean's, May 11/92; p. 29, Report on Business Magazine, June 1990

THE PERSONALS

untying the knot
p. 31, Canada Year Book, 1990

playing it safe
p. 31, Planned Parenthood, 1990, Toronto Star, July 16/90; p. 32, A.C. Nieslen, Toronto Star, March 17/92; p. 32, Today's Health, May/June 91; p. 32, Ontario Medicine, June 22/92

an effort in fertility
p. 32, Today's Health, May/June 1991; p. 32, Toronto Star, April 30/92; p. 33, Globe and Mail, May 19/90

abortion facts
p. 33, Toronto Star, March 13/92; p. 33, Canadian Global Almanac, 1992

STDs
p. 34, Health and Welfare Canada, February 1992; p. 34, Toronto Star, February 1/92

how embarrassing
p. 34, Toronto Star, May 19/90

THE PRICE OF BEAUTY

make-up
p. 36, Today's Health, February 1991; p. 36, Toronto Star, June 16/91; p. 36, Canadian Business, July 1992; p. 36, Toronto Star, August 30/91

makeover
p. 37, Toronto Star, January 14/92; p. 37, Toronto Star, May 24/92; p. 37, Toronto Star, May 24/92, Canadian Society for Aesthetic Plastic Surgery, Globe and Mail, March 7/92

weighing in
p. 37, Ontario Medicine, August 5/91; p. 38, Toronto Star, August 23/90, Toronto Star, April 25/92; p. 38, Toronto Star, August 22/91

WE ARE WHAT WE EAT
Canada's Food Guide
p. 40, Health and Welfare Canada; p. 40, Canadian Grocer, April 1992

the egg comes first
p. 40, Agriculture Canada, Toronto Star, August 18/91

meat market
p. 41, Canadian Hotel and Restaurant, November 1991, Today's Health, June 1991

the dairy case
p. 41, Canada Year Book, 1991; p. 42, Canada Year Book, 1991

getting our veggies
p. 42, Toronto Star, May 23/91, Harrowsmith, November/December 1991, LeisureWays, February 1992, Toronto Star, February 20/92

bringing home the bacon
p. 42, Canadian Grocer, February 1992; p. 43, Canadian Grocer, January 1992; p. 43, Toronto Star, November 10/91; p. 43, Canadian Grocer, May 1992; p. 43, Food in Canada, July/August 1991; p. 43, Canadian Grocer, Executive Report, 1991; p. 44, Canadian Grocer, Executive Report, 1991; p. 44, Chiquita Bananas Canada, 1992; p. 44, Canadian Packaging, December 1990; p. 44, Canadian Packaging, December 1991; p. 44, Canadian Packaging, December 1990; p. 44, Canadian Packaging, February 1992

sweet tooth
p. 45, Toronto Star, January 23/92; p. 45, Maclean's, July 16/90; p. 45, Canadian Grocer, February 1992; p. 45, Canadian Packaging, March 1992; p. 46, Chatelaine, August 1991; p. 46, Statistics Canada, June 1992; p. 46, Globe and Mail, September 8/90

more for your money
p. 46, Allergy Information Association

we'll drink to that
p. 47, ISL International Surveys Ltd., Toronto Star, October 23/90; p. 47, Coffee Association of Canada, Canadian Grocer, November 1991; p. 47, Canadian Consumer, September/October 1991; p. 47, Food in Canada, January 1991, Canadian Hotel and Restaurant, May 1992; p. 48, Food in Canada, January 1991; p. 48, Canadian Packaging, September 1991, Canadian Packaging, February 1992, Cadbury Beverages Ltd.; p. 48, Canadian Packaging, September 1991; p. 48, Promotion Performance, J.G. Inc., Canadian Grocer, November 1991; p. 49, Canadian

Grocer, November 1991; p. 49, Canadian Grocer, Executive Report, 1991; p. 49, Canadian Hotel and Restaurant, November 1991

snack attack

p. 50, Toronto Star, August 7/91, Canadian Packaging, October 1991; p. 50, Maclean's, December 16/91; p. 50, Nestlé Enterprises Ltd., 1991; p. 50, Tootsie Roll of Canada, 1991; p. 51, Report on Business Magazine, December 31/91; p. 51, Dave Nichol's Insider's Report, November 1991; p. 51, Toronto Star, September 28/91; p. 51, Canadian Packaging, March 1992; p. 51, Insider's Report, June 6/92

dining out

p. 52, Health and Welfare Canada, Toronto Star, August 28/91; p. 52, Canadian Hotel and Restaurant, January 1991, Breakfast Television, Citytv, October 28/91; p. 52, Canadian Hotel and Restaurant, November 1991; p. 52, Canadian Hotel and Restaurant, November 1991; p. 53, Canadian Hotel and Restaurant, November 1991; p. 54, Canadian Hotel and Restaurant, November 1991 and June 1991; p. 54-55, Canadian Restaurant and Food Services Association, Globe and Mail, August 8/90; p. 55, Canadian Hotel and Restaurant, November 1991; p. 56, Canadian Hotel and Restaurant, November 1991

under the Golden Arches

p. 56, McDonald's Restaurants of Canada, Report on Business Magazine, April 1991; p. 56, McDonald's Restaurants of Canada, Toronto Star, December 28/91; p. 56-57, McDonald's Restaurants of Canada, Toronto Star, December 28/91, Toronto Star, August 18/91; p. 57, McDonald's Restaurants of Canada, 1990

THE HEALTH OF OUR NATION

health benefits

p. 59, Benefits Canada, February 1992; p. 59, Pharmaceutical Manufacturers' Association of Canada, Toronto Star, December 7/91; p. 59, Health Report, Statistics Canada, Toronto Star, September 14/91; p. 59, Good Times, May 1992; p. 60, Toronto Star, May 28/92

what's up, doc?

p. 60, Ontario Medicine, August 5/91; p. 61, Hospital News, March 1991; p. 61, Toronto Star, October 31/90

take two aspirins...

p. 61, Migraine Foundation, Angus Reid Research, Toronto Star, March 3/92; p. 62, Maclean's, July 16/90; p. 62, Maclean's, July 16/91; p. 62, Ontario Medicine, September 16/91; p. 62, Ministry of Health, Toronto Star, October 3/91; p. 62, Toronto Star, May 14/90

illness, disease and disability

p. 63, Ministry of Health, Toronto Star, November 5/91; p. 63, Ontario Medicine, April 29/91; p. 63, Canadian Medical Association Journal, Toronto Star, January 25/92; p. 63, Medical Post,

October 16/91; p. 63, Canadian Public Health Association, Toronto Star, August 22/91; p. 64, Today's Health, May/June 1991; p. 64, Toronto Star, May 30/91; p. 64, Toronto Star, June 29/90; p. 64, Canadian Paraplegic Association, Toronto Star, February 13/92; p. 64, Toronto Star, May 1/92; p. 65, Maclean's, September 30/91

HIV and AIDS

p. 65, Federal Centre for AIDS, Canada, 1992; p. 65, Toronto Star, October 6/91; p. 65, Globe and Mail, July 12/90; p. 66, Toronto Star, October 7/91; p. 66, Maclean's, April 27/92

surgical manoeuvres

p. 66, Canada Year Book, 1990; p. 66, Chatelaine, April 1992; p. 66, Ontario Medicine, November 1991; p. 66, Saturday Night, April 1991

medical supplies and devices

p. 67, Toronto Star, April 22/91; p. 67, Hospital News, July 1991; p. 67, Toronto Star, July 20/92; p. 67, Canadian Hearing Society

HAZARDOUS HABITS

p. 69, Toronto Star, October 17/90

straight up or on the rocks?

p. 69, Toronto Star, August 8/91; p. 69, Canadian Hotel and Restaurant, January 1992; p. 69, National Alcohol and Other Drugs Survey 1991, Addiction Research Foundation, Toronto Star, December 15/91; p. 70, Report on Business Magazine, February 1991; p. 70, Wine Council of Ontario, Canadian Hotel and Restaurant, May 1991; p. 70, Canadian Business, June 1991; p. 70, Toronto Star, September 24/90; p. 70, Canadian Business, June 1991; p. 71, Maclean's, March 26/91, Report on Business Magazine, June 1991; p. 71, Chatelaine, June 1992; p. 71, Statistics Canada, 1991, Toronto Star, February 13/92; p. 71, Maclean's, June 1/92; p. 72, Canadian Packaging, May 1992; p. 72, Maclean's, July 20/92; p. 72, Canadian Business, June 1991; p. 72, Toronto Life Fashion, April 1990; p. 73, Toronto Star, October 19/90, Globe and Mail, October 26/90; p. 73, Toronto Star, April 25/92; p. 74, Ontario Medicine, June 22/92; p. 74, Toronto Star, February 27/92, Addiction Research Foundation, 1991

illegal substances

p. 74, National Alcohol and Other Drugs Survey, 1991; p. 75, Ontario Medicine, October 14/91; p. 75, Centre for Justice Statistics, 1991; p. 75, Toronto Star, March 18/91; p. 76, Toronto Star, September 25/91; p. 76, Toronto Star, February 27/92; p. 76, Globe and Mail, May 30/92

the smoking section

p. 76, Toronto Star, November 30/90; p. 76, Toronto Star, August 1/91; p. 77, Ontario Medicine, April 6/92; p. 77, Ontario Medicine, February 3/92; p. 77, National Campaign for Action on Tobacco, Toronto Star, October 22/91, Ontario Medicine, February 1992; p. 77, Globe and Mail, May 22/92; p. 78, Canada Year Book, 1991; p. 78, Canadian Business, June 1991; p. 78, Toronto

Star, April 6/91, Maclean's, April 15/91, Maclean's, April 15/91, Toronto Star, April 4/91; p. 78, Globe and Mail, May 22/92; p. 79, Maclean's, April 9/90; p. 79, Globe and Mail, March 14/92; p. 79, Toronto Star, February 27/92

A MATTER OF LIFE AND DEATH

arrivals

p. 81, Toronto Star, April 7/92, Report on Business Magazine, March 1992; p. 81, Statistics Canada; p. 81, Canada Year Book, 1991; p. 81, Canada Year Book, 1991; p. 81, Globe and Mail, March 28/92; p. 82, Toronto Star, March 18/91

departures

p. 82, Canadian Global Almanac, 1992; p. 82, Canadian Mental Health Association, Toronto Star, May 4/91, Quebec Sociologist's Association, Toronto Star, February 20/92; p. 82, Chatelaine, April 1992; p. 83, Statistics Canada, Coroner's Office, 1991; p. 83, Canada Year Book, 1991

the five leading causes of death in Canada

p. 83, Toronto Star, July 16/91; p. 83, Today's Health, May/June 1991; p. 83, Maclean's, April 27/92; p. 84, Canadian Cancer Society 1991, Toronto Star, July 26/91; p. 84, Canadian Global Almanac, 1992; p. 84, Toronto Star, February 1/92; p. 84, Toronto Star, April 13/92; p. 84, Toronto Star, March 18/92; p. 85, Nonprescription Drug Manufacturers Association of Canada, Maclean's, December 16/91; p. 85, Toronto Star, October 25/91; p. 85, Canadian Global Almanac, 1992; p. 85, Journal of Allergy and Clinical Immunology, Toronto Star, July 12/90; p. 86, Canadian Global Almanac, 1992; p. 86, Toronto Star, September 28/90; p. 86, Canadian Global Almanac, 1992; p. 86, The Left-Hander Syndrome, Goodlife, May 1991; p. 87, Statistics Canada, Toronto Star, August 27/91

giving and receiving the gift of life

p. 87, Chatelaine, March 1992; p. 87, Time-Out, Sunnybrook Health Science Centre publication, Red Cross Society; p. 88, Multiple Organ Retrieval and Exchange (M.O.R.E.) Program, Toronto Star, October 11/91

PERSON TO PERSON

telephone directory

p. 90, Statistics Canada, Bell Canada, Toronto Star, July 9/91; p. 90, Northern Business Information, 1989, Toronto Star, June 22/90; p. 90, Financial Post Magazine, August 1990; p. 90, Canadian Automobile Association, Toronto Star, July 26/91; p. 90, Mobile Future, Maclean's, October 14/91; p. 91, Consumer Electronics Marketers of Canada, Toronto Star, March 26/91; p. 91, Toronto Star, May 30/91; p. 91, Toronto Star, July 15/90; p. 91, Canadian Council of Better Business Bureaus, 1991; p. 91, Toronto Star, July 2/90; p. 92, Toronto Star, May 14/90; p. 92, Toronto Star, August 24/91; p. 92, Consumer and Corporate Affairs Canada, Toronto Star, May 17/92; p. 92, Toronto Star, August 24/91

Canada's post
p. 93, Canada Post Corporation, Toronto Star, June 19/91; p. 93, Canadian Direct Marketing Association, Toronto Star, July 9/91, Toronto Star, June 16/91; p. 94, Toronto Star, July 23/91; p. 94, Toronto Star, September 19/90

LEARNING AND LITERACY
learning our lessons
p. 96, Canadian Global Almanac, 1992; p. 96, Canadian Living, June 1992; p. 96, Toronto Star, May 7/91, Financial Times of Canada, March 1992; p. 96, Statistics Canada National Apprenticeship Survey 1990, Toronto Star, March 6/91; p. 96, Toronto Star, May 11/92; p. 97, General Social Survey, Analysis Series, Statistics Canada, Catalogue 11-612E, No. 4; p. 97, General Social Survey, Analysis Series, Statistics Canada, Catalogue 11-612E, No. 4; p. 97, Canadian Global Almanac, 1992; p. 97, Financial Post Magazine, June 1991; p. 98, Toronto Star, May 15/92; p. 98, Report on Business Magazine, June 1992; p. 98, Heart and Stroke Foundation of Canada, 1991; p. 98, MacDonald's Restaurants of Canada, 1990

words without meaning
p. 99, Statistics Canada, 1990, Globe and Mail, June 1/90; p. 99, Conference Board of Canada, 1990; p. 99, Conference Board of Canada, 1990; p. 99, The Creative Research Group, Report on Business Magazine, December 1990

CANADIANS IN NEED
poverty in Canada
p. 101, Canadian Global Almanac, 1992; p. 101, Canadian Global Almanac, 1992; p. 101, Canadian Global Almanac, 1992; p. 101, Toronto Star, February 9/91

feeding Canada's hungry
p. 102, Canadian Association of Food Banks, 1992; p. 102, Toronto Star, September 16/91; p. 102, Canadian Association of Food Banks, 1992; p. 103, Hungercourt Summary, Canadian Association of Food Banks, 1992

the homeless
p. 103, Medical Post, October 1991; p. 103, Toronto Star, April 7/91

charities and volunteering
p. 103, Toronto Star, March 11/92; p. 104, Toronto Star, April 14/91; p. 104, Toronto Star, August 27/91; p. 104, Toronto Star, April 28/92; p. 104, Conference Board of Canada, Toronto Star, June 22/92; p. 105, Time Out, produced by Sunnybrook Health Science Centre, April 1991

helping abroad
p. 105, Foster Parents Plan of Canada, Toronto Star, November 14/91; p. 105, Maclean's, May 20/92

ALL OUR CHILDREN
child care
p. 107, General Social Survey, Analysis Series, Statistics Canada, Catalogue 11-612E, No. 4
baby talk
p. 108, Statistics Canada, Toronto Star, December 4/91; p. 108, Great Expectations, July 1992; p. 108, Canadian Packaging, February 1992; p. 108, National Action Committee on the Status of Women, Canadian Living, March 1992
teen talk
p. 109, Report on Business Magazine, June 1991; p. 109, Canadian Consumer, September/October 1991; p. 109, Decima Research, Addiction Research Foundation of Ontario, Canadian Advisory Committee on the Status of Women, Project Teen Canada, Globe and Mail, May 23/92; p. 110, Chatelaine, May 1992; p. 110, Globe and Mail, May 28/92
child's play
p. 110, Canadian Toy Manufacturers Association, Toronto Star, February 3/91; p. 110, Toronto Star, January 27/91; p. 111, Toronto Star, April 5/92, Report on Business Magazine, July 1992; p. 111, Report on Business Magazine, December 1990; p. 111, Irwin Toy Ltd., 1991; p. 111, Toronto Star, May 5/91; p. 112, Nintendo of Canada Ltd., Toronto Star, December 12/90
latch-key kids
p. 112, Canadian Living, May 1990
the perils of childhood
p. 112, Toronto Star, March 29/92, Toronto Star, July 15/91, Toronto Star, May 30/91, Toronto Star, June 27/91, Toronto Star, September 27/91, Global News, April 3/92, Homemaker's Magazine, October 1991; p. 113, Toronto Star, September 26/91; p. 113, Report on Business Magazine, November 1991; p. 113, Toronto Star, February 10/92; p. 113, Canadian Institute of Children's Health / Toronto Star, May 21/90; p. 113, Globe and Mail, April 18/92; p. 114, Toronto Star, November 5/91
our troubled youth
p. 114, Toronto Star, December 14/91; p. 114, Globe and Mail, May 29/92; p. 115, Canada Year Book, 1990; p. 115, Canada Year Book, 1990; p. 115, Toronto Star, April 4/92

HOME SWEET HOME
the roof over our heads
p. 117, Canadian Home Builders' Association, Toronto Star, February 15/92; p. 117, Toronto Star, July 1/90; p. 117, Canadian Home Builders' Association, Toronto Star, February 15/92; p. 117, Auditor General's Report, 1991; p. 117, Canadian Business, June 1991; p. 118, Environics Research Group, Ltd. of Toronto, Maclean's, April 9/91

creature comforts

p. 118, Toronto Star, February 28/91; p. 118, Department of Industry, Science and Technology Report, April 1992; p. 118, Marketplace, CBC-TV Program, October 22/91; p. 119, Globe and Mail, July 13/90; p. 119, Globe and Mail, April 11/92; p. 119, Report on Business Magazine, August 1992

cleaning up

p. 119-120, Canadian Grocer, March 1991

brushing up

p. 120, Canadian Brush, Broom and Mop Manufacturers' Association, 1992

pet projects

p. 121, Statistics Canada, 1992, Canadian Consumer, September/October 1991, Financial Times of Canada, March 16/92; p. 121, National Animal Health Week, Toronto Star, May 5/92; p. 122, Canadian Kennel Club, 1990; p. 122, Urban Pet Magazine, July 1992; p. 122, Urban Pet Magazine, July 1992

safety begins at home

p. 122, Statistics Canada, Toronto Star, August 27/91

SPORTS AND THE GREAT OUTDOORS

the sporting life

p. 124, Shoe Manufacturers' Association of Canada, Toronto Star, June 29/91; p. 124, Canadian Business, January 1991; p. 124, Toronto Star, June 6/92; p. 125, Maclean's, February 4/92; p. 125, Toronto Star, December 26/91; p. 125, Maclean's, July 27/92; p. 125, Report on Business Magazine, April 1992; p. 125, Global News, May 20/91; p. 126, Financial Post Magazine, June 1991; p. 126, Participaction Ad, Office Systems and Technology, December 1991; p. 126, Toronto Star, July 30/92; p. 126, Toronto Star, August 8/92, Financial Post Magazine, May 1991; p. 127, Maclean's, June 8/92; p. 127, Statistics Canada, Toronto Star, August 27/91

at an average "home game"

p. 127, Toronto Blue Jays, Toronto Star, August 29/91; p. 128, Toronto Magazine, April 1991

dawdling in dinghies

p. 128, Allied Boating Association of Canada, Toronto Star, September 14/91; p. 128, Financial Post Magazine, June 1991

back to nature

p. 129, Chatelaine, August 1990; p. 129, Parks Canada, May 1992, Globe and Mail, May 16/92; p. 129, Toronto Sportsman's Show 1991; p. 129, Canadian Federation of Humane Societies, Toronto Star, December 8/91

GOING PLACES
destination: Canada
p. 131, Canadian Business Life, August/September, 1991, Toronto Star, February 23/91, Canadian Hotel and Restaurant, February 1992; p. 131, Revenue Canada, Toronto Star, August 17/91; p. 131-132, Toronto Star, July 22/91, Canadian Hotel and Restaurant, November 1991, Reader's Digest, February 1991; p. 132, Canadian Automobile Association, Globe and Mail, July 14/90; p. 132, Metro Toronto Convention and Visitors Association, Toronto Star, July 5/91

travelling Canadians
p. 133, Canadian Global Almanac, 1992, LeisureWays, December 1991; p. 133, Canadian Global Almanac, 1992; p. 133, Canadian Hotel and Restaurant, November 1991; p. 134, LeisureWays, December 1991; p. 134, Statistics Canada, Toronto Star, July 18/91; p. 134, Carnival Cruise Lines, Toronto Star, July 30/91; p. 135, Toronto Star, April 23/92; p. 135, Financial Post, July 20/90; p. 135, Canadian Hostelling Association, June 1992

checking in
p. 135, Globe and Mail, January 11/92; p. 136, Globe and Mail, February 22/92; p. 136, Toronto Star, January 16/92; p. 136-137, Royal York Hotel, 1990, Toronto Star, July 11/90, Canadian Business, May 1991; p. 137, Canadian Hotel and Restaurant, January 1991; p. 137, Canadian Hotel and Restaurant, February 1992

tourist traps
p. 137-148, Anne of Green Gables Corporation, Vista, April 1991, Toronto Star, August 18/91; p. 138, Toronto Star, February 1/92; p. 138, Goodlife, May 1990; p. 138, CN Tower, Public Relations, Toronto Star, April 23/92; p. 139, Report on Business Magazine, June 1990; p. 139, Toronto Star, January 21/92, Toronto Star, June 11/91; p. 139, Maclean's, September 30/91; p. 139, Toronto Star, October 3/91; p. 140, Globe and Mail, January 11/92; p. 140, Toronto Star, June 4/91; p. 140, Canadian National Exhibition, 1991

over the border
p. 140, Toronto Star, May 6/91; p. 141, Toronto Star, February 15/92; p. 141, Toronto Star, March 3/91; p. 141, Toronto Star, March 3/91; p. 142, Toronto Star, March 3/91; p. 142, Department of Finance, Tariffs Division, Toronto Star, February 13/92

PLANES, TRAINS AND AUTOMOBILES
airborne
p. 144, Canadian Global Almanac, 1992; p. 145, Toronto Star, July 15/90, Toronto Star, March 16/92, Canadian Global Almanac, 1992; p. 145, Canadian Global Almanac, 1992; p. 146, Statistics Canada, Toronto Star, January 9/92; p. 146, Toronto Star, January 16/92; p. 146, Globe and Mail, February 29/92; p. 146, Aviation and Aerospace, February 1991, Transportation Safety Board of Canada, 1990 Report; p. 147, Toronto Star, March 20/91

on track

p. 147, Toronto Star, January 30/92; p. 147, Maclean's, May 4/92; p. 147, Canadian Safety Council, Railway Association of Canada, Toronto Star, February 13/92

on the road

p. 148, Globe and Mail, August 8/92; p. 148, Report on Business Magazine, September 1991; p. 148, Globe and Mail, March 13/92; p. 148, Report on Business Magazine, June 1992; p. 149, Toronto Star, January 7/92; p. 150, Autofacts Inc., Toronto Star, September 29/91; p. 150, Toronto Star, September 3/91; p. 150, Globe and Mail, May 23/92; p. 150, Canadian Grocer, April 1992; p. 151, Financial Post Magazine, April 1991; p. 151, CBC-TV program, Metro, with Ralph Benmurgui; p. 151, Globe and Mail, March 21/92; p. 152, Toronto Star, September 28/90; p. 152, Toronto Star, February 12/91

public transportation

p. 152, Toronto Star, February 28/92; p. 152, Globe and Mail, May 30/92; p. 153, Toronto Star, April 13/92; p. 153, Toronto Transit Commission, Toronto Star, May 2/91

CRIMINAL ACTIVITIES

crime watch

p. 155, Toronto Star, May 29/91; p. 155, Toronto Star, March 18/92; p. 155, Toronto Star, September 3/91; p. 156, Toronto Star, July 7/91; p. 156, Toronto Star, October 9/91; p. 156, Toronto Star, April 30/91; p. 156, Toronto Star, September 18/90; p. 156, Canadian Jeweller, August 1991

theft

p. 157, Canadian Centre for Justice Statistics, Canadian Mortgage and Housing Corporation, Globe and Mail, April 24/92; p. 157, Maclean's, May 4/92; p. 158, Retail Council of Canada, Style, June 17/91; p. 158, Canadian Centre for Justice Statistics, Toronto Star, July 9/92; p. 159, Canadian Centre for Justice Statistics, Report on Business Magazine, January 1992; p. 159, Toronto Star, September 21/91; p. 159, Toronto Star, May 6/91

offensive driving

p. 159, Canada Year Book, 1990; p. 160, Globe and Mail, April 25/92; p. 160, Toronto Magazine, June 1991; p. 160, PRIDE, Toronto Star, November 9/91; p. 160, Toronto Star, October 31/91

violence against women

p. 161, Health Watch, Fall 1991; p. 161, Toronto Star, May 25/90

elder abuse

p. 161, Toronto Star, April 16/92

behind bars

p. 162, Toronto Star, April 30/91; p. 162, Toronto Star, September 28/91; p. 162, Statistics Canada, Toronto Star, October 9/90; p. 163, Correctional Services of Canada, January 1992; p. 163, Solicitor General's Report, 1992; p. 163, Globe and Mail, April 10/92

gun power

COMINGS AND GOINGS

immigration

the status of refugees

becoming Canadian

Canadians on the move

EARNING OUR KEEP

the working Canadian

money, money, money

p. 180, Bank of Canada, Canadian Living, June 1992; p. 180, Globe and Mail, May 15/92; p. 181, Toronto Star, July 8/90, Toronto Star, July 9/90; p. 181, Globe and Mail, May 9/92; p. 181, Toronto Star, March 6/92; p. 181, Toronto Star, December 7/91; p. 182, Maclean's, July 27/92; p. 182, Maclean's, July 30/91

MINDING OUR BUSINESSES

taking care of business

p. 184, Report on Business Magazine, July 1992; p. 184-185, Report on Business Magazine, July 1992; p. 185, Work Week, April 7/91; p. 185, Maclean's, July 27/92; p. 185, Toronto Star, October 17/91; p. 186, Toronto Star, February 5/92, Toronto Star, January 7/92; p. 186, Canadian Business Life, Summer 1992

command performances

p. 186-187, Report on Business Magazine, June 1992

industrial strength

p. 187, Toronto Star, June 20/92; p. 187, Globe and Mail, June 20/92; p. 188, Canadian Hotel and Restaurant, January 1992; p. 188, Toronto Star, June 24/91

the power of advertising

p. 188, Canadian Association of Advertising, Toronto Star, January 4/92; p. 188-189, Media Measurement Services, Financial Post Magazine, May 1991; p. 189, Maclean's, April 9/90; p. 189, Toronto Star, October 11/91; p. 189, Auditor, Toronto Star, January 24/92; p. 190, Advertisement in Report on Business Magazine, August 1990; p. 190, NCH Promotional Services, Canadian Grocer, Executive Report, 1991; p. 190, Canadian Consumer, September/October 1991, Toronto Star, April 2/91

down on the farm

p. 191, Canadian Global Almanac, 1992; p. 191, Canadian Global Almanac, 1992; p. 192, Canadian Global Almanac, 1992; p. 192, Canada Year Book, 1991; p. 192, Canadian Grocer, October 1990; p. 192, Canadian Meat Council, Canada Year Book, 1991, Toronto Star, September 25/90

cash cows

p. 193, Globe and Mail, May 23/92; p. 193, Toronto Star, September 8/91

bumper crops

p. 194, Canadian Global Almanac, 1992; p. 194, Toronto Star, June 10/91; p. 195, Canadian Global Almanac, 1992

just milling around

p. 195, Canada Year Book, 1991

how sweet it is

p. 196, Canada Year Book, 1991, Canadian Hotel and Restaurant, May 1992; p. 196, Canada Year Book, 1991; p. 196, Canada Year Book, 1991

fire alarm

p. 209, Canada Year Book, 1990; p. 209, Canada Year Book, 1990; p. 210, Canada Year Book, 1990; p. 210, Globe and Mail, May 29/92; p. 210, Canada Year Book, 1990; p. 210, Maclean's, December 25/90

energy, mines and resources

p. 210, Canadian Global Almanac, 1992; p. 211, Canadian Global Almanac, 1992; p. 211, Canadian Global Almanac, 1992; p. 211, Harrowsmith, November/December 1991; p. 211, Canadian Global Almanac, 1992; p. 211, Canadian Global Almanac, 1992; p. 211, Canadian Global Almanac, 1992; p. 211, Globe and Mail, April 10/92; p. 212, Canadian Global Almanac, 1992

TIMBER!!!!!!!!!!!!!!!!!!!!!!!

p. 213, Toronto Star, July 15/92; p. 213, Pulp and Paper Industry of Canada, Report on Business Magazine, December 1990; p. 213, Maclean's, December 16/91; p. 214, Toronto Star, October 28/90; p. 214, Report on Business Magazine, October 1991; p. 214, Pulp and Paper Journal, July 1991; p. 214, Harrowsmith, November/December 1991; p. 214, Pulp and Paper Industry of Canada, 1990, Maclean's, July 16/90; p. 215, Canadian Pulp and Paper Association, Report on Business Magazine, October 1991; p. 215, Globe and Mail, June 30/90; p. 215, Toronto Star, January 21/92; p. 215, Statistics Canada, 1990; p. 215, Canadian Green Consumer's Guide, Toronto Star, June 20/91; p. 216, Toronto Star, May 11/92

catch of the day

p. 216, Department of Fisheries and Oceans, Canada Book of Facts, 1992; p. 216-217, Department of Fisheries and Oceans, Canada Book of Facts, 1992; p. 217, Canada Year Book, 1991; p. 217, Department of Fisheries and Oceans

trappings

p. 217-218, Canadian Global Almanac, 1992; p. 218, Globe and Mail, June 8/91

animal research and testing

p. 218, Canadian Council on Animal Care, Toronto Star, April 16/91

BUY, SELL, TRADE

imports/exports

p. 220, Canadian Global Almanac, 1992; p. 220, Globe and Mail, May 23/92

trading partners

p. 221, Canadian Global Almanac, 1992; p. 222, Canadian Global Almanac, 1992; p. 222, Canadian Global Almanac, 1992; p. 222, Report on Business Magazine, August 1990; p. 223, Toronto Star, May 27/91; p. 223, Maclean's, June 29/92; p. 223, Toronto Star, August 13/92; p. 223-224, Toronto Star, August 13/92; p. 224, Toronto Star, July 19/91; p. 224, Toronto Star, July 19/91

specialty trade

p. 225, Toronto Star, July 8/90; p. 225, Report on Business Magazine, November 1991; p. 225, Financial Post, July 3/90; p. 225, Project Carvingstone, NWT Government, Globe and Mail, July 18/90; p. 226, Globe and Mail, June 20/92; p. 226, Toronto Magazine, June 1990

what's in store?

p. 226, Toronto Star, May 25/91; p. 226, Canadian Grocery Bag Manufacturers' Association, 1991; p. 226, Maclean's, February 3/92; p. 227, Toronto Star, October 22/91; p. 227, Maclean's, March 27/90; p. 227, Canadian Grocer, August 1991; p. 227, Toronto Star, May 15/91; p. 227, Toronto Star, June 16/91; p. 227, Canadian Direct Marketing Association, Globe and Mail, July 18/92

if the shoe fits. . .

p. 228, Shoe Manufacturers' Association of Canada, April 1990; p. 228-229, Shoe Manufacturers' Association of Canada, April 1990; p. 229, Shoe Manufacturers' Association of Canada, April 1990; p. 229, Style, October 15/91; p. 229, Toronto Star, December 2/91; p. 229, Toronto Star, August 24/91

fashion statement

p. 230, Financial Post, July 23/90; p. 230, Alex Tilley, President, Tilley Endurables; p. 230, Toronto Star, April 7/91; p. 230, Canadian Jeweller, October 1990; p. 231, Toronto Star, April 21/92

high tech

p. 231, Toronto Star, June 5/92; p. 231, Toronto Star, July 6/92; p. 231, Maclean's, November 27/91; p. 231, Toronto Star, August 24/91

GOVERNMENT AND POLITICS

the feds

p. 233, Toronto Star, April 13/91; p. 233, Statistics Canada, Canadian Grocer, March 1991; p. 233, Toronto Star, March 13/92; p. 234, Auditor General's Report, 1991; p. 234, Toronto Star, November 2/91; p. 234, Maclean's, June 29/92; p. 234, Globe and Mail, October 26/91; p. 235, Report on Business Magazine, April 1992; p. 235, Toronto Star, July 20/92; p. 235, Toronto Star, June 16/91; p. 235, Toronto Star, February 2/91; p. 245, Toronto Star, October 11/91; p. 236, Toronto Star, October 19/91; p. 236, Statistics Canada; p. 236, Statistics Canada, Toronto Star, August 29/91; p. 236, Toronto Star, December 24/91; p. 237, Toronto Star, April 30/90

the GST

p. 237, Burns Fry Ltd., Toronto Star, March 3/92; p. 237, Toronto Star, May 3/91; p. 237, Toronto Star, April 9/91

the price of politics

p. 238, Toronto Star, July 14/92; p. 239, Toronto Star, July 14/92; p. 239, Elections Canada, Toronto Star, July 16/91; p. 239, Elections Canada, Toronto Star, July 16/91

dear sir

p. 240, Toronto Star, November 2/91; p. 240, Toronto Star, April 14/92

OPINION POLLS

the inside scoop

p. 242, Gallup Canada, Toronto Star, May 11/92; p. 243, Gallup Canada, Toronto Star, July 6/92; p. 244, Gallup Canada, Toronto Star, July 6/92; p. 244-245, Gallup Canada, Toronto Star, July 6/92; p. 245, Gallup Canada, Toronto Star, July 27/92; p. 245, Gallup Canada, Toronto Star, June 30/92; p. 246, Gallup Canada, Toronto Star, June 22/92; p. 247, Gallup Canada, Toronto Star, May 21/92

would you believe?

p. 247, Gallup Canada, Toronto Star, October 31/91; p. 248, Toronto Sun, July 8/91

on the outside looking in

p. 248, Angus Reid Poll, May 1992; p. 249, Angus Reid Poll, May 1992; p. 249-50, Angus Reid Poll, May 1992, Toronto Star, May 16/92

ABOUT THE AUTHOR

Heather Brazier has overcome some remarkable odds to write this, her first book. In 1990 she made the news by graduating from York University with a degree in English Literature. Her studies were complicated by major medical problems—including spina bifida and a severe lung disease—and took almost 10 years to complete. Heather, a writer and an avid collector of statistics, lives in Toronto.